Women Brickmakers from Cradley Heath — see page 25
Reproduced by permission of Birmingham Central Library
Local Studies Department

2

A FEAST of MEMORIES
BLACK COUNTRY FOOD AND LIFE AT THE TURN OF THE CENTURY

by Marjorie Cashmore

A Commemorative terra cotta plaque built for Queen Victoria's 1897 Jubilee

PUBLISHED BY

Westwood Press Publications

PRINT SHOP, 44 BOLDMERE ROAD, SUTTON COLDFIELD
WEST MIDLANDS   TELEPHONE 021-354 5913

For

My Family and Friends

WARNE'S MODEL COOKERY

HINTS TO HOUSEKEEPERS

On the Lady of the house devolves the task of providing food for her household; it should be her care that no waste or ignorant misuse shall squander the property of her husband—most frequently the bread-winner for the family—and that nothing is lost by carelessness or bad cookery. She is to take care that there is no lack through fault of hers, nor any drawback to domestic comfort through injudicious rule; no neglect caused by the love of idle pleasure.

© Copyright 1986, Westwood Press and the Author

1st Edition September 1986
Reprinted Autumn 1988
Reprinted December 1993

Printed and Published by The Westwood Press
44 Boldmere Road, Sutton Coldfield, West Midlands B73 5TD
Produced by offset litho.

4

Contents

Reproduced from the Cannon Iron Foundries trade catalogue of October 1908

Acknowledgements

I am indebted to the many wonderful Black Country people, too numerous to mention who have willingly shared their memories and recipes with me and to those who have generously loaned treasured family photographs, the owners of which are credited in the captions.

I also wish to express my thanks to Cannon Industries for their permission to reprint a selection of holloware and logos taken from old trade catalogues.

Particular thanks go to my Father in-law Reg, Tom Hobley and Jim Harcourt, friends of my late father who talked to me about their unbelievably strict childhood, youth, and life-long service in the local furnaces and Rowley Rag stone quarries. Despite a rough up-bringing, these hard-working people, typical of working-class folk of their era, have led active lives well into their late seventies and eighties, suggesting perhaps that the humble diet outlined in the following text was adequate and helped sustain them in their work.

My special thanks go to all my colleagues, past and present at the Black Country Museum, in particular Ian Walden for allowing me to reprint photographs and posters from the Museum archives, Stuart Holm, John Crompton, Sean Smith, Noel Ashley, David McDougall, Gayner Iddles and Wendy Turner for their involvement and to Diane Willetts and Cheryl Carpenter who helped with the typing.

Finally, I am indebted to my family and close relations and friends for their support and encouragement. To my husband and brothers David and Peter for providing valuable information, to my daughter Jan and sister Pat for their heroic efforts in helping to check and test the recipes, and to my son John who designed the cover and illustrations.

My thanks to you all.

Family group — The Reverend Noott, his family and congregation celebrating the Golden Jubilee of St. John's Church, Kates, Hill, Dudley

High Street Dudley, 1893

Foreword

Marjorie Cashmore's family have been part of the Black Country for a century and a half. Her great grandfather, the Reverend Edward Henry Lane Noott, the youngest son of a Cardigan doctor, settled in Tipton as a curate and in 1844 was offered the living of the newly created parish of St. John, Kate's Hill, Dudley. The Church then was surrounded by cornfields and green meadows but the view from the Vicarage overlooked Tipton with its scores of blast furnaces, and in a letter written in 1844 by Dr. Thomas Noott whilst visiting his son in Dudley, he referred to the sight of the country around "all on fire" and described how his room at night was lighted by the "fires two miles away as if one of the new gas lamps has been fixed outside my window".

The Reverend Noott's concern for the plight of his poorer parishioners and his genuine respect for all Black Country folk is evident from accounts of his life. He became so committed to his adopted homeland that he remained at Kate's Hill for the rest of his life though he doubtless had opportunities to move on to less taxing rural parishes. He married a sister of the local ironmaster Sir Alfred Hickman and subsequent marriages linked the Noott line with many local families great and small so that Marjorie can claim descent from ironmasters and clergymen, colliers and teachers.

As a child, Marjorie mixed freely with local people from all walks of life. Already her keen eye was subconsciously absorbing scenes which were to become incorporated in this book and she was getting to know the shopkeepers, quarrymen, factory workers and housewives who would later supplement her own vivid memories of the Black Country diet and way of life in the last generation before television and the electronic age plunged the region into a new period of transition and change.

Marjorie started collecting recipes long before she conceived the idea for this book. Many were passed down from relatives and friends in the traditional way and sustained her family as they had fed

9

generations before. She was fortunate in having the means to obtain quality ingredients and the skill to prepare them properly. As a result, while many of her contempories were rejecting the traditional dishes with their connotations of hardship and poverty, they continued to find a place on her table alongside the more cosmopolitan dishes of the new age.

When the wheel turned full circle and people began to tire of convenience foods and look back with nostalgia to the days when food had flavour without additives, Marjorie was saddened to find that faggots and peas and groaty pudding seemed to be overshadowing the wealth of other fine Black Country dishes which she appreciated so much. Once her love and experience of cookery was known to her colleagues at the Black Country Museum she was, on occasions, called upon to prepare traditional meals for museum functions where she became increasingly aware of the need to dispel the strenghtening myths about local food and so the idea for this book was born. As she began supplementing her own store of recipes with those gleaned from friends and acquaintances she found that conversation that began on the subject of food, invariably released a flood of memories of a bygone age and so it seemed natural to include some of these memories as an accompaniment to the food.

The historical reminiscences help place the recipes in context but Marjorie's main purpose in compiling this book was to introduce the taste of traditional Black Country cooking to a new generation. It is also a heartfelt tribute to the achievements of the women of the Black Country. Their kitchens were the forgotten workshops whose products sustained the great industries for which the area is perhaps better known. If historians feel inspired by these pages to embark on a more systematic study of life in the Black Country it is to be hoped that they will first go out and buy a few pounds of pig's liver or a beef's cheek and, with the aid of this book, make themselves a meal which, to quote Marjorie's own words, will "sustain them in their labours".

Stuart A. Holm
January, 1986

Introduction

I am often asked to provide recipes for the three dishes most commonly associated with the Black Country, namely, Faggots and Peas, Groaty Pudding, and Bread Pudding. These nourishing and filling meals often appeared at the table of working-class families, at the turn of the century but it would be wrong to suppose that little else was eaten. In order to dispel this widely held misconception, I have endeavoured to gather together in this volume a collection of recipes passed down through my own family and those drawn from the recollections of elderly people good enough to provide me with such rich and varied accounts of their childhood in the late eighteen and early nineteen hundreds. The recipes collected from these sources were popular then but are unlikely to have received much attention in subsequent years, the region having been recognised more for its industry than its cuisine.

A great deal of my research was conducted in the warm atmosphere of local pubs, full of character and characters, some of whom very kindly invited me to visit them in their own homes. These meetings often took place in cosy old dwellings, the contents and style of which provided a revealing insight into the social activities of earlier times. Whilst in the company of these friendly and warm-hearted people, the conversation inevitably turned to vivid accounts of their childhood and youth, a time spent without the materialistic trappings of today's society, but nevertheless extremely interesting and varied, embellishing some of the darker years of our history.

In order to share some of these reflections with the reader, I have interspersed my collection of recipes with a little social history, providing a glimpse of a way of life now so dramatically changed. This additional information is not intended as an academic historical survey but rather as a complementary record of how Black Country people ordered their everyday lives in the late eighteen and early nineteen hundreds, frequently coping with very limited resources. The self-sufficient ingenuity developed by these people was nowhere better displayed than in the kitchen where humble ingredients were transformed into tasty and nourishing dishes, some of the older and more unusual of which are included here.

Marjorie Cashmore

ST. THOMAS'S PARISH.

PENNY MEALS.

The Vicar has arranged to provide Penny Dinners for the destitute at the Guild Rooms.   Tickets for distribution can be had at the Vicarage.   About 200 poor are fed daily from 11-45 till 12-30.

Secretary—Miss Gerrie, The Vicarage.

Reproduced from the Dudley Almanack

Pit Bank Wenches

The Black Country

It is said that whilst travelling by train through the Black Country, Queen Victoria requested that the blinds of her carriage windows be drawn, the ravaged landscape being too obnoxious to witness. Whether this actually occurred is questionable. What is relevant, however, is the scene which was evolving beyond those windows during the queen's reign. Amidst the squalor and filth of this landscape, constantly shrouded in a canopy of smoke and steam, and resounding with the din of industrial toil, there was emerging a race of people, destined, through their skills and craftsmanship to be ensnared in the turmoil of expansion and growth following the Industrial Revolution, the outcome of which was to help shape the future history of the entire world.

This once rural isolated plateau of the ancient Kingdom of Mercia, with its verdant, densely-wooded landscape and crystal-clear streams, ravaged now beyond recognition, came to be known as the 'Black Country'. The name derived not only from the grime and dirt pouring from the many furnaces and chimney stacks which mushroomed over the landscape and polluted the air with noxious gasses, but also from its wealth of coal, in places occurring up to thirty feet thick. To exploit this thick seam of coal, many pits were sunk. Colliers mined underground, women known as [pit bonk wenches] or [booney wenches] sorted coal at the screens above ground and children led the pit ponies or worked the ventilation doors. The unsparing hand of the miners rapidly left the ground honeycombed and scarred.

The exact boundaries remain arguable but the Black Country can be conveniently defined as the region to the West of Birmingham, lying between Wolverhampton, Walsall, Stourbridge, and Halesowen, encompassing an area approximately ten miles square. Abundant in mineral resources, coal, ironstone, fireclay and limestone, the Black Country soon became acclaimed throughout the world for its superb craftsmanship in the manufacture of iron products and the breed of people carrying out these skills were renowned for their tenacity,

Map of The Black Country

courage, generousity, warm-heartedness and not least of all, their droll sense of humour.

The accent and intonation of voice of Black Country people have long been a source of amusement to outsiders but the dialect in fact derives from Anglo-Saxon with noticeable Chaucerian affinities and is considered by some to be the purest form of English. Being essentially a spoken tradition, the Black Country accent does not easily lend itself to translation into print but in the following text where the pronunciation varies significantly from standard English, phonetic spellings are given in square brackets.

A distinctive feature of many Black Country people is the ability to laugh at themselves, often applying a humorous approach to a serious subject, but as jokes and anecdotes tend to lose their meaning if not spoken in the vernacular, they may not always be appreciated or understood by anyone unfamiliar with the dialect and ways of Black Country people.

Black Country Sheet Iron Rollers.

Heavy chain making in The Black Country — B.C.M.

Scene at the Pit Head, alongside the Boiler — B.C.M.

Life today in the Black Country is a far cry from that at the turn of the century, when the social conditions of the working classes, although much improved by comparison with the earlier years of the Industrial Revolution, were barely tolerable. A noticeable chasm existed between the rich and the poor, and poverty, squalor and illiteracy prevailed. Every winter took its toll and deaths from cold and malnutrition were common. Men, women and children were compelled to work unbelievably hard in an effort to earn a meagre living; ironfounding and forging, brick-making, mining, quarrying, leather-working, lock-making, enamelling, glass-blowing, etcetera. To enable these families to work long hours at their skills, simply prepared but nourishing and filling dishes were provided by housewives. Meals consisting of relatively cheap ingredients which improved with slow-cooking were left to simmer on a hob at the side of the fire whilst the entire family was working.

"The Woodall Team", glass marking ready for engraving
—Dudley Reference Library

Black Country people enjoyed similar types of meals as their fellows throughout industrial Britain and familiar dishes such as Steak and Kidney Pudding, Rabbit Stew and Roly Poly Pudding to name but a few were very popular and commonly referred to as 'rib-stickers'. Most of the recipes given here, however, are believed to represent typical Black Country variations. Also included are a few simple inexpensive remedies for minor ailments, using herbs and plants which, despite the harsh environment, grew in abundance in the meadows and lanes surrounding Black Country hamlets.

These recipes have been drawn from all sections of the Black Country and reflect the difference from family to family: poorer families using cheaper cuts of meat and food they had available at the time. Ingredients were rarely measured and with no controls on the ovens, cooking became a skill. The correct temperature for baking bread for instance was determined by popping a sheet of newspaper inside the oven and if it turned brown in a few seeconds, was an indication that the oven was hot enough. Ingredients were measured out in cups and spoons, and whilst most women used a wooden board for chopping and preparing food, the more affluent had hand-operated mincing machines which were clamped down to one edge of the kitchen table and proved invaluable for mincing ingredients. With no refrigerators and freezers, food was kept cool on the shelves at the cellar head or on the sills below which provided an adequately cool storage area even on the hottest day.

Many children subsisted on a diet of hunger-allaying concoctions (bally-fillers) which would confound todays' dieticians but because of renewed appreciation of regional food in recent years, a few of the methods have been adapted using modern techniques and contain ingredients which many working-class families at the turn of the century could ill-afford. It will be noticed that plain flour and baking

Small Chain Shop at Noah Hingley's, Netherton — B.C.M.

Miners setting a pit prop—By kind permission of Basil Poole

powder were called for in most of these old recipes, but I personally find that self-raising flour gives a much lighter texture. Similarly, cooking oil could replace lard for frying purposes and I find vegetable suet is a splendid alternative to beef suet. Otherwise, most of the recipes are best left in their original form to retain the correct flavour. The inclusion of these up-to-date ingredients, however, may tempt more affluent generations to sample humble traditional Black Country dishes.

Three Favourites

[A Boungin o 'Bostin Fittle]

The waste-heaps of the coal mines [pit bonks] were a useful, free source of fuel for poor families. Men, women and children could often be seen 'picking coal' for their own use, especially during trade recessions and strikes. Old prams or hand-carts known as 'dobbins' were used to carry the coal away and each year, just before 5th November, 'bonfire night', children were busy collecting lumps of inferior coal known as 'bats'. These were used as the foundation for their bonfires which often burned for days. Families gathered around the fire where basins of Groaty Pudding were eaten, with baked potatoes cooked in the cinders and only raked out and considered to be ready for eating when a thick charcoal-like crust had formed on the skin.

GROATY PUDDING
[Grauty Pudding or Grauty Dick]

½ lb Groats*
1½ lbs shin of beef (cut into bite-size pieces)
1lb leeks (sliced)
2 medium-sized onions (sliced)
1 Bay leaf (optional)
Hot water to cover
Salt and pepper

(Sufficient for four)

---

* Groats are a cereal. When milled for human consumption, oats are first cleared of any weed seeds, or small stones and then kiln dried and stored for twenty-four hours before the outside husk can be removed. In this form they are known as groats and are subsequently ground to produce oatmeal. Rolled oats are made by steam cooking groats before rolling them into flakes. Groats are more extensively used for animal foods, but are equally good for human consumption, having the highest nutritional value of any of the cereals.

Oval Boiling Pot

21

Place all the ingredients in a stew jar or casserole dish and bake slowly for at least three hours, longer if possible, when this dish will be comparable with any meat and vegetable casserole, and much tastier than the name implies. Serve with crusty bread. A thicker version of this with more groats and less meat was all some families could provide. It was spread on bread so that each member could have something warm and filling.

FAGGOTS AND PEAS

[Faggits and Pays]

1½ lbs Pig's fry
2 medium-sized onions
2 tablespoons fresh sage or
1 tablespoon dried sage
1 cup of fresh breadcrumbs
Salt and pepper
1 tablespoon plain flour or cornflower mixed with a little water for thickening the gravy.

(Sufficient for four)

Thoroughly wash the fry leaving the caul* [kell] in lukewarm water as this makes it more pliable to handle later. Mince or chop the fry and onion and mix thoroughly with the breadcrumbs, seasoning and sage. Form into eight portions and wrap each portion in a piece of caul. Place in a baking dish and cover with water. Bake in a moderate oven for about three hours, basting frequently until the faggots are nicely browned. More hot water can be added if needed during basting. Thicken the juices half an hour before serving. Faggots are traditionally served with 'mushy peas'—dried peas soaked overnight and then steamed or slowly boiled while the faggots are cooking. An alternate version for faggots is to boil the fry for a short time prior to mincing or chopping; either way produces tasty faggots.

---

* Caul is the lacy fatty membrane surrounding the stomach and gut of the pig and forms the outer coating of the faggots, keeping them moist during cooking.

BREAD PUDDING
[Fill Bally]

2 lb stale bread
½ lb shredded suet
1 lb granulated or brown sugar
1 lb mixed dried fruit
3 eggs
2 oz butter or margarine
2 teaspoons mixed spice

Soak the bread in water and then drain and squeeze out the excess moisture. Flake with a fork and add the remaining ingredients. Mix well together and spread the mixture into a greased baking tin. Dot with butter and bake in a moderate oven for about two hours or until nicely browned. A variation of bread pudding is a pastry base spread with a little jam, covered with a thick layer of the above mixture and baked in a medium oven. As the name implies, this dish helped to fill the childrens' bellies and also utilised any crusts of stale bread, as "waste not, want not" was the order of the day.

Typical Victorian Schoolroom

Shop — Typical Black Country 'front room' shop

Caring for a Family

[No plaerce like wum]

Caring for a family at the turn of the century was far from easy. Men worked long hours to provide for their families, and many working-class women, besides rearing their children also helped supplement the family income by making nails and chain, brick-making, taking in laundry or sewing, or even converting their 'front' rooms into shops, selling anything from sweets to lamp oil in an effort to make a little extra money.

In the little ramshackle oddwork shops, known in some areas as [tungitts], at the rear of most working-class houses, women made chain alongside their husbands and other members of the family during the day and could still be found working late at night, singing "Britains never shall be slaves"! The extra chain they made was stored by some women in their peaked cloth caps until the following morning—a

Women brickmakers at Cradley Heath — By kind permission of Dudley Library

capful being considered a fair quantity to make in an evening. A woman's pay, however, was only about one third of that paid to a man. Although infant mortality was very high it was common for a woman to have a child every twelve to eighteen months until often there would be twelve or more children to feed, clothe and care for. There was certainly no fear of working-class women suffering from upper-class ennui.

In the straggling rows of terraced houses, there were plenty of bare, frugal households but home was a refuge and families pulled together to improve the quality of their lives, making every effort to rise above the squalor, and camouflage the underlying poverty. The kitchen or 'back' with its distempered walls was the main living area in 'two up, two down' working-class homes. It was here that the family gathered to read, sew, iron, cook, eat,

Shoe Last

mend footwear on a three-footed last and of course take their once weekly bath in a zinc tub in front of the fire.

Reproduced from the Dudley Almanack

The room had a profusion of necessities for the family from tea in a huge japan-ware caddy on the mantlepiece, to the family bible on the chest of drawers; from homemade newspaper spills with which Father lit his pipe, to a line slung between opposite walls close to the fire, to air clothes. This room was usually kept spotlessly clean. The table, the window ledges and the settle, usually known as a 'screen' or 'squab', were scrubbed regularly and the red quarry-tiled floor was scrubbed or mopped daily with soda water with a little ochre powder or raddle added to help retain the colour of the tiles. This was occasionally followed by a wipe over with a little sour milk, giving a final glaze.

The room was lit by either candle light, oil lamps or gas lamps; the first being hardly adequate, the second messy and requiring regular cleaning to be efficient, and the third creating a minor catastrophy if

Meat Jack

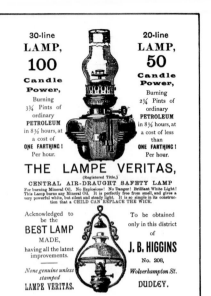

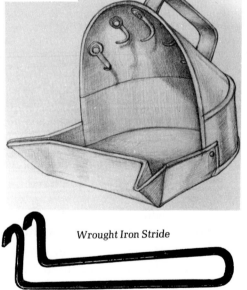

Dutch Oven

Wrought Iron Stride

the gas mantle happened to get broken. The wooden scrubbed-topped table in the centre of the room was where food was prepared and eaten and family activities such as reading, sewing and ironing took place. If gas was installed, it was here, over the table that the gas lamp hung. The insanitary conditions of the day harboured flies and in order to protect food, sticky fly-papers were hung close to the light to trap invading insects. Jugs and basins containing food and milk were covered with round crocheted mats with glass beads sewn around the edges to act as weights.

The focal point of this room was the black-leaded grate with its open fire providing heat, and hobs on either side for food and water to be left simmering. There was also a side oven for baking and roasting. Food could be fried over the open fire in a frying pan which hung on an S-shaped gale hook from an extending arm called a 'crane' but a popular method of cooking was with a 'Dutch Oven', or 'Toaster' which was placed on a pair of 'strides' attached to the front bars of the firegrate. A Dutch Oven has a flat base with a semi-circular heat reflector at the back, bearing hooks from which bacon, sausages, etcetera can be hung and cooked in front of an open fire.

Joints of meat were also cooked in front of the fire on an implement called a 'Meat Jack', 'Bottle Jack' or 'Spit'. This is a clockwork device from which the meat is hung and which rotates backwards and forwards, enabling the meat to be evenly cooked. These of course were the forerunners of todays rotisseries. A roasting tin placed on the strides caught the juice which was then used to baste the meat as it cooked. Beef with plenty of fat was the popular choice as this provided the family with 'dripping' which, when cold and spread on bread was a meal in itself. Food cooked this way was especially succulent even though one or two embers [gledes] would have to be retrieved from the baking tin from time to time. Less affluent families not possessing a Meat Jack would improvise with a back door key and a length of string twisted sufficiently to wind and unwind, enabling the meat to rotate exactly as on a Meat Jack.

With such large families, meals were taken in relays. The menfolk, who were considered the main 'bread winners' always ate first and were served the largest helpings. It was common to see children sitting on door steps or on the pavements outside their homes, eating their dinner in the form of a chunk of bread dipped in gravy with potatoes spread on top and if they were lucky, a little meat. At intervals throughout the day, chunks of bread with a variety of toppings such as treacle, dripping, condensed milk or jam were eaten as a substitute for meals, and were just known as a 'piece',

The fireguard or 'fender' was also put to good use for quickly drying out washing or rain-soaked clothes and shoes. The leather shoes of course, being dried too close to the fire became very hard and cracked and took days to break into the mould of the foot again. The owners of this distorted footwear no doubt complained but they were always aware how lucky they were to possess shoes at all, as bare-footed or badly-shod children were a common sight at that time.

Gale Hook

Because of the multi-purpose nature of the grate, a fire was necessary summer and winter and last thing at night, particularly in the winter, a piece of coal known in the Black Country as a [rareka], was placed on the fire and backed up with coaldust known as [slack] or [sleck], creating a damper effect. In the morning, air was introduced by raking out the ashes and in no time, with the use of a draw plate or a sheet of newspaper a welcoming fire was roaring away and water bubbling in the kettle which had been left on the hob overnight.

Hearty breakfasts were considered a necessity as this ["lined ya bally for the day"], and generous slices of homefed bacon or ham were soon sizzling in the Dutch Oven or frying pan. If the supply of bacon was running low, the younger members of the family often had just thick slices of bread dipped in the licquor. These were known as pieces of dip or [dooer stops]. Horse-drawn milk floats toured the streets every day. Women carrying jugs

Milk Measure

8th FEBRUARY 1893

Fatal Colliery Accident at Hart's Hill—three miners named Aaron Crew. Joseph Jones, and John Oliver precipitated to the bottom of the pit shaft.

Reproduced from the Dudley Almanack

gathered around the floats, many of them having only enough money to purchase half a gill measure of milk, ladled with the appropriate measure from the churns. Few children experienced drinking milk in large quantities and eggs were similarly scarce, one egg often being shared, but a substantial breakfast sufficient for several children could be made using the following recipe.

Hanging Frying Pan

EGGY FINGERS

Thick slices of bread
1 egg
A little milk
Salt and Pepper
Lard or dripping

Beat the egg with the milk, salt and pepper, dip thick fingers of bread into the mixture and fry them on either side in hot dripping or lard. These are also an excellent accompaniment to a mixed grill.

Empty sugar bags and even old shoes were filled with slack, dampened and placed on the back of the fire to "slow it down". The ashes fell into an ash pan in the 'ess hole' or 'perkitt hole' which was regularly cleaned out and the gledes re-riddled; the bigger ones to be re-cycled again as fuel, the remainder used to bed down paths around the house and garden and the remaining fine ash tipped in the ash pit behind the privy. "Old Glede" was also a term used scathingly to describe an old woman and another apt expression when describing a raucous voice was "like a glede under a door".

Fire grates were cleaned with 'black lead' which was purchased in block form, mixed to a paste with water, often in an empty half coconut shell and then vigorously rubbed into the metal work until it shone like polished jet. Cleaning these grates was a thankless chore but most housewives reserved part of one day each week to clean them, helping to create a warm, cosy atmosphere.

A fringe made from chenille but known as 'plush' adorned the edge of the mantle shelf. Some women were lucky enough to have a matching tablecloth but newspaper or oilcloth were more frequently used as a table covering at mealtimes. A floor to ceiling cupboard filled the alcove between the firegrate and the outer wall. This is where treasured possessions such as best crockery and ornaments were stored on shelves edged with fancy cutout shaped newspaper trim, but enough room was sometimes made available in the bottom section for the cat to rear her kittens.

Furniture was sparse in most houses but nearly every family possessed a chest of drawers. The top drawer was reserved for storing important items such as a purse, the rent book and insurance policies, the drawers below for towels and clothing. Nothing was wasted in any form and old jackets, trousers and skirts, already having been passed down from the older members to the youngest and no longer serviceable as garments were washed and cut into strips approximately three inches by one inch. These were then woven into a piece of hessian sack [erdan bag] with the aid of a 'podger', an implement designed to push [podge] the cloth between the weave of the hessian. A double tuft resulted which eventually transformed these oddments of old material into a brightly coloured and cosy rug. Where a podger was not available, a wooden clothes peg broken in half, made a good substitute. Care was taken to work the strips into attractive designs as these rag-rugs on the hearth were often the only floor covering. They were very heavy but the dirt and dust was shaken from them daily on the backyard or 'fold' [fode]. A rug of this type was usually made every year in time for Christmas, but less affluent families often had to resort to using them as a bed covering to provide extra warmth in the winter.

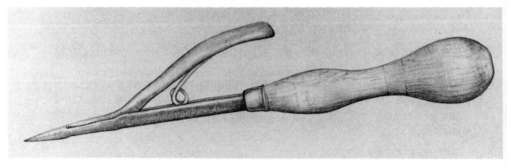

Podger

Women kept to a strict routine with their household chores, each day being allocated to a specific job. Ironing was done with a 'flat' or 'sad' iron which was heated on the strides in front of an open fire, the flat under-surface being gently spat on to test if it was hot enough to use. If the spit sizzled and bounced off quickly, the iron was hot enough. Two irons were used simultaneously; one in use, the other heating in front of the fire which had to be kept sufficiently hot even in the hottest weather.

Sad or
Flat Iron

Iron Stand

It was fashionable for younger female members of the family to wile away the long winter evenings round the fire, making samplers. Intricate embroidered stitches were lovingly woven into an oblong of material, depicting scenes, special events, or family trees, and the girl working the cloth always embroidered her name and age at the foot of the sampler, on completion. The few surviving ones have now become collectors' items. An iron or kettle holder was always a useful item for children to make as they were used regularly in the kitchen and frequently needed replacing.

Corking

Girls and boys alike practiced 'corking' which was generally referred to in the Black Country as girdling. Using a spent cotton reel which in those days was made of wood, four small nails were hammered into one end at equal distances from the centre hole. Wool was then wrapped around the nails and with a darning needle or knob pin, the bottom layer was hooked over the top layer. After working several rounds in this manner it was possible to pull the growth of girdling through the hole in the reel, the finished result resembling a length of cylindrical knitting. Children spent endless hours using up oddments of wool into yards of unevenly-striped lengths of corking which were then stitched together to make mats or slippers of a kind.

33

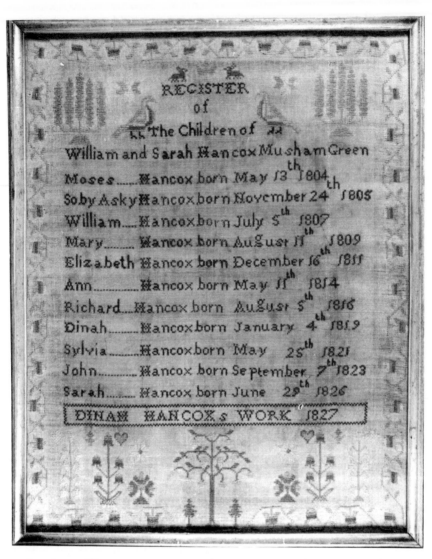

REGISTER
of
The Children of
William and Sarah Hancox Musham Green

Moses_____Hancox born May 13th 1804
Soby Asky Hancox born November 24th 1805
William_____Hancox born July 5th 1807
Mary_____Hancox born August 11th 1809
Elizabeth Hancox born December 16th 1811
Ann_____Hancox born May 11th 1814
Richard_____Hancox born August 5th 1816
Dinah_____Hancox born January 4th 1819
Sylvia_____Hancox born May 25th 1821
John_____Hancox born September 7th 1823
Sarah_____Hancox born June 29th 1826

DINAH HANCOX's WORK 1827

Sampler—William Hancox, son of John Hancox, owned a chainshop in the Mushroom [Musham] Green area of Cradley Heath and in his heyday employed about eight men on a permanent basis and had many outworkers. The sampler, now in the possession of the Author's sister who married into the Hancox family was completed by Dinah in 1827, aged eight years

The same type of wooden reels were used by boys as 'tanks'. Grooves were cut on the outer edges of the reel and an elastic band threaded through the centre hole. The elastic band was secured at either end by match sticks and when wound sufficiently, the 'tank' charged across the table, wiping out whole battalions of enemy en-route. Imaginery battlefields were rigged up and boys fortunate enough to have toy soldiers were kept amused for hours on end, unaware that the soldiers and their covering of paint contained lead and were, therefore, highly dangerous. Sisters were rarely invited to join in these 'battles' but sat quietly observing or keeping score. Fretwork was another popular past-time for boys, and younger children played 'houses' under the table or scribbled in chalk on the backs of the screens. At bedtime, with just the light from an open fire and perhaps the warm glow of an oil lamp, children gathered around the hearth to look for 'pictures' in the flames. This proved very relaxing at the end of a busy day and soon induced sleep.

There was no indoor sanitation in houses of this type, the privy, (sometimes known as petty, or closet), being housed at the end of the tiny garden, beyond the coalhouse which adjoined the brewhouse. These were two or three seater open closets with wooden lids to cover the hole when not in use. Behind the closet was the ash pit into which all the fine ashes from the fire were tipped as these absorbed the effluent from the closet. The ash pit regularly required cleaning out by workers known as night soil men or [night silers] because they carried out their unsavoury occupation at night. Any surplus newspaper not required for lighting fires or to substitute as a table cloth was cut into neat squares and threaded with string to serve as toilet paper.

With a limited number of bedrooms, several children slept together in one large bed, toe to toe, the baby of the family often sleeping snugly in a clothes basket or even the bottom drawer of a chest of drawers. Iron bedsteads with hard, lumpy straw or flock mattresses were the type of beds most working-class people slept on; feather beds being considered an enviable luxury. To heat the bed in winter a housebrick was placed in the

Stoneware Hot Water Bottle

Hop-picking Kiln and Yard — see page 82

oven and when heated through, was wrapped in a remnant of blanket or old clothing and placed in the bed instead of the stoneware hot water bottle which warmed and aired the beds of the more affluent families. Chamber pots were hidden under the beds for use during the night and the Black Country term for these was [guz unders] or [po's].

With no bathroom facilities, a matching decorative jug and bowl were placed on a washstand in the bedroom for ablutions. Cold water was carried upstairs in these jugs each evening for use the following morning but an alternate luxury was the warm water from the water bottles. Children, however were 'topped and tailed' from an enamel bowl on the table downstairs in front of the fire and on cold winter mornings most of the family did the same, the only alternative being the sink in the brewhouse or the pump on the [fode]. It was more practical for men to wash and change from their working clothes in the evening and again this was done in front of the fire in the kitchen or brewhouse, before they sat down to eat.

Connecting the two downstairs rooms was a small cellar where most of the perishable food was kept on the stone sills and in meat safes. Shelves at the cellar head were also used for storing crockery and kitchen utensils.

Lipped Maslin Kettle

Round Frying Pan

A pungent, damp, musty smell lingered in the front room of most houses of this type through lack of ventilation and heat, as this room, always referred to as 'the front', was rarely used except for weddings and funerals or when the vicar called. When a death occurred in the family tradition dictated that the coffin containing the corpse was placed there until the day of the funeral, to allow relations, friends and neighbours to call and pay their last respects. A heavy curtain was hung over the front door which opened straight into this room from the pavement outside, but most of the time, newspaper was packed into the crevices to prevent draughts and dust penetrating.

With dark brown brush graining on the woodwork, cumbersome antimacassar-draped furniture and the numerous large pictures covering much of the walls, the overall effect would seem rather over-powering by today's standards but home management and decor was greatly influenced by the middle-class attitudes of the day. Consequently, with little use being made of the room, the furniture was hardly sat on but the popular aspidistra plant, thrived in this dark, clammy atmosphere.

Horse & Cart — By kind permission of Jim Aldridge.
Taken in Church Road, Rowley Village, Rowley Regis, at the turn of the century

Black Country Decorating

The following method of decorating a room at the turn of the century was taken from a hand-written note book belonging to a Black Country woman, the late Miss Muriel Powell who must often have used this method during her lifetime.

The Ceiling

Wash off the old whitewash with hot water to which has been added a little borax. Use an old sponge and do not damp it too much. Let this dry. To make whitewash, make it just as advised for distemper, but add a little laundry blue to make it dead white instead of any colouring.

Walls

Put a pound of whitening into a bucket and pour on enough boiling water to make it into a thin paste. Add one pound of size which has been melted down slowly in an old saucepan. Mix well, colour if you want it pink with a little red ochre, or if you want it deep cream, with a little yellow ochre. Add the colours very slowly until you get the right tint. Finally, add a tablespoon of powdered alum and stir well. Set aside until the distemper is cold, when it will be like a thin jelly. Dust the walls down well. Take the distemper on the brush and brush down the walls from the ceiling to floor. Keep doors and windows shut, otherwise it dries too quickly and shows the marks of the brush. Don't put on the distemper too thickly. Put it on thinly and then you can always put on another coat if it does not cover enough, but you will be surprised when the distemper is dried to find how little it takes to cover the walls. Don't judge if your work is nice until the walls are quite dry.

10th JANUARY 1893

Death of a young woman named Sarah Ann Jones at Gornal Wood on the 10th and of her grandmother Hannah Jones on the 14th through inhaling carbonic acid gas which escaped from the coal seams below the houses in which they resided.

Reproduced from the Dudley Almanack

Vegetables

[Tairters, Passnips and Pays]

Families fortunate enough to have a garden, allotted most of the ground space to growing vegetables to help supplement their diet, with perhaps a small border for herbs, flowers and rhubarb. Most families kept a patch of horseradish, as the root was a popular accompaniment to beef, but not made into a sauce, merely scraped with a very sharp knife into slivers and stored in an earthenware pot with a cork stopper. A little at the side of one's plate is sufficient as it is exceptionally hot, but a small quantity added to gravy gives an agreeable piquancy.

Another popular plant which took up very little space in the garden but which is sadly neglected by the majority of today's gardeners was the tree onion which has a unique flavour and is extremely good in bread sauce and stuffings. Sliced, boiled beetroot with the addition of seasoning and a little melted butter was a popular second vegetable. Although most vegetables were eaten as they came into season, some, like runner beans were salted down for use during the winter months.

Nearly everyone made their own pickles which included onions, red cabbage, beetroot, walnuts and damsons. Chutneys, sauces and piccalilly were also popular ways to use up bumper crops. Pickles were stored in wide-necked earthenware jars, often with the fresh bladders of newly-killed pigs serving as a cover. These bladders were stretched over the top of the jar and allowed to dry to the exact shape, thereby forming an airtight lid. At the end of the sprout-picking season, the stalks were not dug up and discarded but were left in the ground until new shoots appeared in the spring. These greens were then boiled gently for about five minutes and served with a slice of homefed ham or bacon. A drop of vinegar sprinkled over the greens enhanced this dish. Boiled cabbage and bacon was a similar meal, both recipes being easy to prepare but very satisfying. Meals incorporating vegetables were relatively plain but the following recipes are a little more unusual.

STEWED PARSNIPS AND CELERY

2 large parsnips
2 sticks, finely-minced celery
A little milk
Salt and pepper

(Sufficient for four)

Dice the parsnips and boil them in a little water until tender. Drain, season with salt and pepper and place them in a saucepan with the celery. Pour over a little boiling milk, cover closely and stew slowly for about fifteen minutes. Serve as a second vegetable.

TURNIP SOUP

6 turnips
1 cup of sago
1 pt. milk
A knob of butter
Salt and pepper
1 pt. of stock

(Sufficient for four)

Clean and dice the turnips and boil in a little water until tender. Drain then mash or sieve them. Gradually add the stock, and season with salt and pepper. Gently simmer the sago in the milk until the sago is soft, then add to the mashed turnips. Add a lump of butter and simmer for a further ten minutes.

BEETROOT SAVOURY

1 onion
3 medium-sized beetroot (boiled and diced)
2 tablespoons wine vinegar
Salt and pepper

(Sufficient for four)

Slice the onion and fry in a little butter. Add the beetroot, season with salt and pepper and add the vinegar. Cook until tender and serve hot on buttered toast.

STEWED CELERY

2 heads of celery
1 pint of milk
Salt and pepper
1 oz cornflour

Wash the celery well and cut into one inch lengths. Place in a saucepan with the milk and simmer for about thirty minutes. Thicken with cornflour and season with salt and pepper. Serve with meat, fish or poultry as a second vegetable.

PARSNIP BALLS

1 finely mashed parsnip
1 dessertspoon of melted butter
1 dessertspoon of milk
1 beaten egg
Fresh breadcrumbs
Salt and pepper

(Sufficient for two)

Mix throroughly together the parsnips, butter, milk, salt and pepper and form into balls. Egg and breadcrumb and shallow fry them until golden brown. These are a good accompaniment to beef.

STUFFED MARROW AND TOMATO SAUCE

1 large vegetable marrow
approx 1 lb. minced beef or bacon
1 large onion minced or chopped
2 tomatoes (skins removed and flesh chopped) —
Salt and pepper
Dripping or cooking oil for frying
¼ lb cheese

(Sufficient for four)

Cut the marrow in half lengthwise and discard the seeds. Fry the onion in dripping until soft, and brown the meat. Add tomatoes, herbs and a little stock if necessary to bind ingredients together. Fill the cavities of the marrow with the mixture and cover with a layer of grated cheese. Bake in a moderate oven for about two hours or until the cheese is golden brown and the flesh of the marrow soft. Alternatively, the marrow can be boiled for about half an hour before adding the filling which reduces the baking time to about one hour and ensures that the flesh of the marrow is tender.

ST. THOMAS'S CHURCH OF ENGLAND TEMPERANCE SOCIETY.

The Band of Hope meet in the Central Schools, King Street, at 6-45 on Monday Evenings. Secretary, Mr. T. Wright-Hill.

A REGISTER FOR THE UNEMPLOYED.

The Vicar keeps a Register for unemployed parishioners, in the hope of finding work for them. Applications may be made at the Guild Rooms at 10 a.m. daily.

WOOD CHOPPING FOR THE UNEMPLOYED.

Men out of work may earn their dinner by wood chopping, or they may earn dinners and further relief for those dependent upon them by work in the labour sheds connected with the Guild Rooms No parishioner need starve with hunger, but every one able to work must be prepared to work if work can be found, otherwise they may not eat of the bread of charity.

Reproduced from the Dudley Almanack

SAUCE FOR STUFFED MARROW

1 lb fresh tomatoes or 1 large tin
1 small onion
1 clove of garlic (optional)
small knob of lard or 1 tablespoon vegetable oil
1 pint chicken stock
2 teaspoons wine or malt vinegar
1 tablespoon of cornflour
1 bouquet garni made from the following herbs:
A sprig of marjoram
A sprig of parsley
1 small bay leaf

Fry the onion and garlic in lard or oil until soft then add the remaining ingredients. Boil gently for about twenty minutes and put through a strainer. Thicken with cornflour mixed to a paste with a little water and continue simmering gently for about five minutes. Cut the marrow into four portions and pour the sauce over. Serve with crusty bread and butter.

GRIDDLE POTATO

Thinly sliced potatoes
Thinly sliced onions
A little grated cheese
Seasoning

Grease a griddle or frying pan liberally with dripping or lard and cover the base with a layer of potatoes overlapping in order to completely cover the bottom of the pan. Cover with a layer of onions and the grated cheese. This dish was cooked either on a griddle over the fire or baked slowly in the oven for about one hour.

Shocking Suicide by John Green (35), of Oldbury, by hanging

Reproduced from the Dudley Almanack

SAVOURY PUDDING

3 large onions
4 oz shredded suet
4 oz fresh breadcrumbs
1 teaspoon thyme
1 teaspoon sage
1 beaten egg
Salt and pepper
1 oz dripping
(Sufficient for two)

Boil the onions in a little water until tender. Drain well, chop finely, add all the ingredients except the dripping and mix well. Heat the dripping in a pudding basin and cover with the savoury mixture. Bake in a moderate oven for about one hour. Serve with crusty bread and butter.

LEEKS AND BACON (Method 1)

Thoroughly clean required amount of leeks, slice and gently fry them in bacon fat. Serve with grilled ham or bacon. (Leeks can be par-boiled before frying if preferred).

LEEKS AND BACON (Method 2)

Thoroughly clean, slice and boil required amount of leeks until tender in a small amount of milk and water. When cooked, thicken with cornflour and water, add a small knob of butter and serve with grilled bacon and boiled potatoes.

SWEDE AND POTATOES

Boiled swede and potato, mashed together with a little butter and served with beef steak was very popular and often just the mashed swede and potato would be served on bread as a main meal when the family budget didn't run to meat. Parsnips were an alternative to swedes.

SWEET BEETROOT PICKLE

6 medium-sized beetroot
2 onions
2 teaspoons dill seed
12 fl. oz wine vinegar
½ teaspoon salt
1 teaspoon dry mustard
9 oz sugar

Boil the beetroot until tender and set aside until cool. Remove the skin and slice into rings. In a medium-sized saucepan combine the vinegar, mustard, salt, sugar and water together and bring to the boil. Remove the saucepan from the heat and set aside. Arrange the beetroot slices and onions in layers in clean, screw-top jars. Add the dill seed and cover with the hot vinegar solution. Tightly screw the tops of the jars, cool and then place in the refrigerator. Allow to stand a few days before serving. This pickle will keep well for several weeks in a refrigerator.

ELDERBERRY SAUCE

2 quarts elderberries
2 quarts vinegar
3 blades of mace
1 small piece bruised root ginger
1 dessertspoon cloves
2 dessertspoons peppercorns
4 large shallots or onions
3 oz demerara sugar

Strip the elderberries from the stalks using a fork. Place them in a casserole dish with the sugar and cover with a lid. Cook in a very slow oven for about twelve hours. (This was usually left in the oven overnight). Pour off the liquid and put in a saucepan with the vinegar, mace, ginger, peppercorns, cloves and finely chopped shallots or onions. Boil for about ten minutes. Pour this liquid over the berries again and bottle all together. Cork securely. When required, the liquid should be drawn off the berries. This sauce is very versatile as it can be served hot or cold with any roast or boiled joint of meat or poultry.

POTATO SQUARES

Slices of cold meat
Cold mashed potato
1 egg
Parsley
Mustard
A little milk for glazing

Beat the egg and mix with the mashed potato. Spread the slices of meat with mustard and cover them on both sides with the mashed potato. Place them in a greased dish, brush the tops with the milk and bake in a medium oven for about half an hour. Sausage was sometimes substituted for meat. This was an economical way of using up left-over food.

POTATO SPLITS

4 oz plain flour
1 teaspoon baking powder
6 oz mashed potato
¼ pint of milk
2 oz lard
1 teaspoon salt

(Sufficient for two)

Mix together the flour, salt and baking powder and rub in the lard. Lightly mix in the mashed potato. Mix to a soft dough with the milk. Roll out to ½ inch thickness then cut into rounds. Bake in a moderate oven for about twenty minutes. When cold, cut through to make a sandwich with shredded vegetables mixed with mayonnaise, gravy, or sauce.

2nd JANUARY 1885

Annual Treat to aged poor and widows of Cradley, by Miss Hingley, in Cradley High Town Ragged School

FEBRUARY 1885

Fifth Entertainment in aid of the Soup Kitchen Fund, in the Public Hall, Sedgley

Fifth distribution of Soup and Bread to the distressed poor, at Sedgley

---

Reproduced from the Dudley Almanack

POTATO SAUSAGE ROLLS

Potato Pastry (page 97)
¼ lb sausage
Seasoning
3 oz mashed potato

Skin the sausages and mix with the mashed potato and seasoning. Prepare the pastry and roll out into a long strip. Roll the filling into a long length, using a little flour. Place on the pastry, damp the edges and roll up, pressing the edges well together. Cut into three inch lengths with a sharp knife. Bake in a moderate oven for about twenty minutes.

MEAT AND VEGETABLE PIE

Potato Pastry (page 97)
4 oz minced meat
2 carrots
2 potatoes
2 tomatoes
Bunch of watercress
A little cabbage
A little cauliflower
Stock and seasoning

(Sufficient for two)

Prepare the vegetables, dice the carrots and potatoes, slice the tomatoes and shred the cress and cabbage. Arrange in layers in a pie dish with the meat and season well. Cover with potato pastry. Bake in a medium oven for about one hour.

———————

Herbs were also gathered, dried and stored in readiness for the winter. A pinch of the following mixture was sufficient to flavour any soup, stew, or recipe requiring mixed herbs:

Dry and crush into powder from the following herbs: mint, parsley, thyme, powdered mace, clove, lemon balm, black pepper, cayenne and two bay leaves. Mix all together thoroughly and store in tightly stoppered jars.

Pig-Killing

[Evathin but tha sqwale]

Before the days of mass-produced food, people relied largely on their self-sufficiency. Pigs were an important family asset and relatively easy to rear. They were fed on a diet of pig-swill consisting of pig-meal (ground cereals) made into a paste with boiling water, 'mashed' and then diluted to a thinner consistency with cold water. Stale bread was added to this together with previously boiled potato peelings. Pigs were usually fattened ready for killing just before Christmas, sustaining the family and supplementing their diet throughout the year.

Pig-killing, always a gruesome, gory affair was considered quite an event and children and adults alike joined in the occasion. The Pig was held down on a wooden trestle (a form of bench known in some areas as a 'cratch'), by several men, one standing at the head of the pig, which would be on its back at this stage with a rope noose secured around its snout. The pig's head was jerked back in readiness for the 'sticking' when a knife was plunged swiftly into the pig's jugular vein. There was usually someone skillful enough to perform this task in most villages but people with several pigs would seek the help of a professional slaughterer or local butcher. Today, pigs are humanely killed, i.e. stunned before being 'stuck' but in those days were dragged from the sty to the backyard or 'fold' [fode], often escaping and running wild before being re-caught and dragged to the bench squealing with fright; perhaps they somehow sensed the fate that awaited them.

Immediately the pig had been slaughtered the carcass was scalded with hot water, the bristles scraped away from the skin and then thoroughly cleaned. Slits were cut in the skin at the back of the hind feet revealing the strong sinews, and a strong piece of wood wedged through the two, enabling the pig to be hung from huge hooks which were a standard feature in most kitchens or brewhouses at this time, specifically for this purpose. Whilst hanging in this position, the pig's carcass was slit open and the innards caught in a large pan known in the Black Country as a [mill pon]. A bowl was then placed under the snout to catch any remaining blood and the carcass was left for several days to drain, during which time full use was made of the offal. Nothing was wasted—even the bladder [blether] was used for covering jars of pickles, or by the children as a football. The trotters, tail and pig's head were utilized, together with the heart, kidney, liver, lights, sweetbreads, caul, leaf and intestines and the following are some of the nutritious and mouth-watering recipes which Black Country folk made from pigs.

Reproduced from the Dudley Almanack

BONEY PIE

[Booney Pie]

When the meat had been jointed, the remaining bones were not discarded but were transformed into a robust pie. The bones, liberally covered with meat, were chopped into manageable pieces and placed into a large basin. A little stock or water and seasoning was added and a funnel placed in the centre of the dish. A pastry lid was carefully placed over the bones and then cooked slowly in a medium oven for about one hour. This pie was eaten either hot or cold and needed only the addition of mustard to make a hearty meal. Alternatively, the pork bones were boiled beforehand.

SAUSAGES

(Stuffed Gut)

Surprisingly, one of the culinary delights at pig-killing time was a particular dish made from odd pieces of meat left over when the pork had been jointed and the bacon and hams cut ready for salting. These scraps of pork were minced or chopped finely and, with the addition of a little minced onion, sage, thyme and a few breadcrumbs, were stuffed into the 'gut' section of the intestines which had of course been scrupulously cleaned beforehand. The sausage was then sewn up and baked slowly for about one hour, producing a delicious aroma. These were the forerunner of todays commercially-made sausages, but far superior in flavour to the majority.

CHITTERLINGS

[Chittalins]

Chitterlings are the smaller intestines of the pig. These were thoroughly cleaned several times in running water and then plaited to make them more compressed. They were boiled in salted water for several hours and left to cool, when they were served with bread and butter and a sprinkling of malt vinegar. Alternatively, boiled chitterlings were cut into small pieces and fried with sliced onions in a little butter. Stock was then added and the dish left to simmer for a while. The gravy was thickened with flour or cornflour just before serving.

SWEETBREADS

Sweatbreads are the glands found in the neck and stomach of pigs, calves, bullocks and lambs, and were regarded as a delicacy in the nineteenth century more so than today. Lambs' sweetbreads are the finest in texture but pigs' sweetbreads were more readily available to Black Country people. They have a surprisingly delicate and rich flavour and are very filling. It is important to soak them in cold water for several hours before removing the skin and any membranes. This renders them white and firm. Place the prepared sweetbreads in a pan of cold water, bring to the boil, remove the pan from the heat and set aside for ten minutes before draining. The sweetbreads are then ready to fry or braise. The following recipes illustrate ways in which the more affluent members of Black Country society used sweetbreads.

FRIED SWEETBREADS

2 Sweetbreads
1 egg
Fresh white breadcrumbs
Stock
A little fat for frying

Prepare the sweetbreads as above and simmer in stock for about forty minutes. Drain, brush with egg, coat with breadcrumbs and fry in hot fat until nicely browned. These were popular served on fried bread.

BRAISED SWEETBREADS

2 Sweetbreads
½ pint white sauce
A few mushrooms
Rounds of toast

Gently saute the mushrooms and add to the sauce. After initial preparation of the sweetbreads, slice them, place them on the toast and serve with the mushroom sauce poured over.

BRAWN

First thoroughly clean the pig's head, cover with water and boil for about two hours until the meat falls easily off the bones. Chop the meat finely, add salt, pepper and a sprinkling of nutmeg and mix well. Put the mixture into a basin with a saucer placed on top. Place a weight on the saucer to compress the meat mixture and leave in a cool place overnight until set.

CHAWL

(Pig's cheeks)

Chawls are usually cured at the time of pig-killing for use later when they should be first soaked overnight and then baked in the oven as a joint or made into potted meat.

STUFFED PIG'S EARS

The pig's ears are soaked for about five hours, covered with fresh water and simmered for about two hours. A filling of forcemeat made from breadcrumbs, suet, parsley, thyme, salt, pepper and beaten egg is packed into the pig's ears which are then secured with thread and lightly fried. After poaching them gently in stock for about one hour they are served with a sauce made from the stock and eaten with bread and butter.

PIG'S FEET AND EARS

Thoroughly clean four pig's feet and ears and place in a saucepan with an onion, a blade of mace and the rind of a lemon. Cover with stock or milk and simmer until tender. The feet and ears are then cut into small pieces and a sauce made from the stock. Combine the pieces of meat with the sauce and heat thoroughly before serving.

Opening of the New Workhouse Schools, Shaver's End
Inquest on the body of Henry Southwick (33), of Cradley Heath, who was scalded to death at the Corngreaves Works—Verdict, "Accidental Death"

Reproduced from the Dudley Almanack

PIG'S FEET AND TAILS

A substantial meal can be made from pig's feet and tails, pearl barley, onions and dried peas, boiled together for several hours and served with boiled potatoes. They can also be eaten cold with a little vinegar sprinkled over.

SOUSED PIG'S FEET

2 Pig's feet
1 teaspoon salt
¾ pint vinegar
¼ pint stock
6 pepper corns
A little allspice
4 cloves
A little mace

Scald and thoroughly clean the pig's feet, cover with water, bring to the boil and simmer them until the meat easily comes away from the bones, removing the scum as it rises. When they are cooked, place them in a dish and cover them with the vinegar and the measured amount of the stock in which they are cooked. Add the salt, pepper, spice, cloves and mace and cover them closely. Leave overnight. This dish is usually eaten cold.

SAVELOYS

3 lbs of pork
½ lb cooking salt
½ oz saltpetre
2 teaspoons pepper
6 sage leaves (chopped)
½ lb fresh breadcrumbs

Remove the skin and bone from the pork and rub the meat with the saltpetre and salt. Let it stand in the brine for three days then finely mince it and season with pepper and sage. Add the breadcrumbs and mix all well together. Fill skin bags with the mixture and bake them in a slow oven for half an hour. They may be eaten hot or cold.

The following recipe was an unquestioned way of making Black Pudding at the turn of the century, but for obvious reasons is now unacceptable.

PIG'S PUDDING
(Black Pudding)

A quart of blood caught in a vessel when the pig is killed
1 quart of groats
1 loaf rubbed into breadcrumbs
2 quarts of milk
1 teaspoon each of thyme and winter savoury
2 teaspoons salt
1 teaspoon pepper
6 cloves
½ teaspoon allspice
½ nutmeg (grated)
A little grated ginger
3 pounds of shredded suet
6 eggs (beaten)
3 ounces pork fat (diced)

Stir the hot blood with salt until it is quite cold. Add the groats and leave to soak overnight. Soak the breadcrumbs in the milk, previously heated, and add the salt and pepper, herbs, eggs, suet, allspice, cloves, ginger and nutmeg. Combine with the groat mixture and mix well. Put into skin bags, adding pieces of fat at regular intervals. Tie the skins in links only half-filled, and boil the puddings in a large saucepan, pricking them as they swell to prevent them bursting. When boiled, dry them in clean cloths and hang them up. Pig's Pudding can be eaten cold or fried.

Fatal Accident to Thomas Stanton, of Ball Street, Gornal Wood, by falling from a skip to the bottom of a pit at Old Fields, Lower Gornal.

Reproduced from the Dudley Almanack

BAKED PIG'S FRY

1½ lbs fry (minced)
1 large onion
1 teaspoon chopped sage
2½ lbs potatoes
¼ teaspoon pepper
1 teaspoon salt

(Sufficient for four)

Boil the onion and combine with the sage. Lay half the fry at the bottom of a pie dish, cover it with a thin layer of sage and onions, sprinkle it well with pepper and salt, and cover it with a layer of sliced potatoes. Repeat with the remaining ingredients ending with a layer of potatoes. Cover with water and bake in a slow oven for about two hours. Towards the end of cooking time, dot the surface with butter and continue baking until the top is nicely browned.

PIG'S LIVER CASSEROLE

1 lb pig's liver
1 lb potatoes
¼ lb onions
A pinch of fresh or dried sage
Salt and pepper
½ pint of water

(Sufficient for two)

Wash and dry the liver and cut into slices. Slice the onion and potatoes. Place them in a greased dish, season with salt and pepper, a little sage and enough water to cover. Place greased paper on top and bake slowly for about two hours.

LIVER HOT POT

1 lb potatoes
1 lb pig's or lamb's liver
2 onions
1 large cooking apple
Plain flour
1 teaspoon dried sage
Salt and pepper

(Sufficient for four)

Peel and slice the potatoes to about half an inch thickness. Slice the liver into half inch strips and coat with the seasoned flour. Peel and chop the onions and apple and mix with the sage. Put layers of potato, liver, onion mixture, and salt and pepper in a greased casserole dish, ending with a layer of potato. Pour over a teacupful of boiling water, cover with a lid and bake in a medium oven for one hour. Remove the lid and cook for a further half an hour until the potatoes are nicely browned.

PORK SAUSAGE PUDDING

1 lb Pork sausage
Puff pastry
Salt and pepper
Dry mustard
Sage

(Sufficient for four)

Butter a large pudding basin and line it with pastry. Prick the sausage with a darning needle and place in the basin with a seasoning of salt, pepper, dry mustard and a suspicion of sage. Pour in a little water, cover with a pastry crust and bake in a moderate oven for about an hour.

KIDNEY PUDDING

2 pig's kidneys
2 teacups breadcrumbs
1 teacup suet
1 teacup milk
A little nutmeg & parsley
Salt and pepper
Beaten egg and milk

(Sufficient for one)

Skin the kidneys and mince finely. Add the remaining ingredients, mix well and steam for about one hour.

Inquest on Richard Turner(18), a Miner, of Old Hill, who died from the effects of being struck by a tub in the workings at the Eagle Colliery.

Reproduced from the Dudley Almanack

BRAINS AND EGG

2 sets of pig's or sheep's brains
2 eggs
Salt and pepper
(Sufficient for two)

Clean the brains thoroughly in salt water and poach for about fifteen minutes. Poach or boil the eggs and mix with the brains. Add salt and pepper to taste and serve with thinly cut bread and butter. This dish was served to invalids to help them regain their appetite, as it was particularly easy to digest. Brains, par-boiled and then fried whole in bacon fat and served with bacon was also very popular.

PIG'S HEAD

At the end of the week, butchers sold off very cheaply or gave away what meat they had left over, usually offal or the cheaper cuts known as 'scrag-ends' or 'kag-mag'. Although the following recipe would be considered rather messy by the majority of cooks today, lots of families relied on these hand-outs and made full use of them. The pig's head, which was usually chopped into manageable pieces by the butcher, was put to soak in water for a few hours and then thoroughly cleaned, the brains being reserved for use later. The head was then boiled in salted water for about two hours, the meat removed from the bones and served hot with vegetables and a sauce made from the brains. The sauce was a basic white sauce with the addition of parsley and the brains previously boiled and chopped and was considered a suitable dish to serve to invalids. Sheeps's heads were cooked and served in a similar way.

ST. THOMAS'S PARISH.

GRIFFITHS' CHARITY.

By her Will (dated 29th January, 1873), the late Miss Rebecca Griffiths gave to the Vicar and Churchwardens of St. Thomas's Church, Dudley, a sum of money sufficient to produce £50 per annum, to be distributed in clothing to poor working people of respectability in the parish of Dudley. Tickets are given away in December, and the recipients then select the clothing they require from the shops of local tradesmen, who are paid by the Vicar.

Reproduced from the Dudley Almanack

BACON CURING

One of the most skilled and time-consuming tasks after pig-killing was the curing of bacon and hams. Methods varied but if curing was not properly carried out, the result was bacon and ham which very quickly turned sour [reesty]. In fact, some men would only have a pig slaughtered when there was a [waxin mewn], believing that the bacon would not cure properly if the moon was on the wane. The carcasses were taken to the cellar and laid on the sills for dry-curing. A carcass weighing sixteen to twenty score (twenty pounds) required twenty-eight pounds of salt and eight ounces of saltpetre. The skin was singed to remove hairs and bristles and the carcass cut into pieces, removing the head and the chine, with some of the back meat and the ribs. The sides of bacon were cleaned by sprinkling the flesh side with salt and rubbing salt into the skin. They were left to drain for twenty-four hours, flesh side down, then wiped with a clean cloth. Saltpetre was sprinkled on the flesh side of the shoulders and hams and half the salt sprinkled over the sides which were then placed one on top of the other. After seven days the remaining salt was added and the position of the sides reversed. They were left to cure for about four weeks and then wiped and hung up to dry for seven days after which they were cut into hams, middles and shoulders, wrapped in calico or muslin cloths and then brown paper and hung up to dry around the living room walls. Black Country people referred to these sides of bacon and hams as 'pictures' and treasured them more than they would any great work of art.

GREY PEAS AND BACON

(Grey pays and bearcon)

1 lb dried grey peas
3 oz pearl barley
1 lb bacon
A large sliced onion
Salt and pepper
(Sufficient for four)

Soak the peas and pearl barley overnight and then place in a saucepan together with the onion, previously browned bacon and salt and pepper. Cook slowly for several hours. This dish can also be cooked in a pressure cooker. (Bacon pieces are much cheaper and can be purchased from some grocers or butchers).

BAKED LIVER AND BACON

1 lb sliced liver
½ lb bacon
1 large minced onion
Fresh breadcrumbs
Salt and pepper
Chopped parsley

(Sufficient for four)

Grease a baking dish and add half a cup of water. Lay the slices of liver in the dish and cover with the onion, salt, pepper and plenty of bread crumbs mixed with the chopped parsley. Cover this with slices of bacon and bake in a moderate oven for about half an hour.

LIVER AND BACON PIE

1 lb thinly sliced liver
3 rashers of bacon
1 large onion
3 lbs of cold mashed potatoes
Salt and pepper
1 oz butter

(Sufficient for four)

Grease the bottom of a pie dish and cover with layers of onion, liver, bacon and potatoes. Season each layer, ending with a layer of potatoes to form a crust. Pour a little water over the ingredients before the final layer of potato, roughly decorate with a fork and dot with butter. Cook slowly in a medium oven for about one hour.

MAY 1900

14 — Death from Enteric Fever of Private S.H. Clarkson of Dudley Ambulance Corps, at Orange River Camp, South Africa.

18 — News of the Relief of Mafeking was received shortly after 10 o'clock on the night of the 18th May, and very soon vast crowds of people assembled in the Market Place and other parts of the Borough.

Reproduced from the Dudley Almanack

A SMALL BAKED HAM

Soak the ham for twelve hours, changing the water several times. Dry it thoroughly and cover it with greased paper. Make a paste with plain flour and water and roll it to cover the ham over the paper. Place on a baking tin and bake in a moderate oven for about three hours. Remove from the oven and crack the paste which will be very brittle. Remove the paper and skin which will come off very easily and to impart a delightful flavour, squeeze over it the juice of an orange. Eat hot or cold.

To give a special flavour to a boiled ham or bacon, add a cupful of vinegar and six cloves to the water whilst cooking, letting it remain in the stock overnight. Remove from the stock in the morning and set aside in a cool place to become firm before serving.

Hams were often steamed in the boiler in the brewhouse. The boiler was filled with cold water and the ham lowered into it together with a bunch of fresh herbs (parsley, marjoram, thyme and sage), tied in muslin. The ham was boiled for forty minutes, the fire raked out and the ham allowed to remain in the boiler overnight, covered with a closely fitting lid, to keep in the steam.

HOMEFED LARD

Lard was made by rendering down the 'leaf' (known in some areas as 'flead') of the pig, which is the fatty membrane surrounding the kidneys and loin. This was cut into small cubes and together with some of the rind, rendered down very slowly in a large saucepan or mazzling kettle. As the leaf was reduced, the melted fat was poured into containers to set, with a few sprigs of rosemary sprinkled on top to give added flavour. The resulting lard was then used for frying food, for pastry and cake making, and also for spreading on bread or toast as an alternative to butter. The crisp, crunchy pieces of fat remaining in the pan were thoroughly drained and eaten as 'scratchings' and bore no resemblance to the scratchings sold commercially today. With a little salt sprinkled on them, they were very tasty and completely edible.

Fashions in Clothing

[Up fust, best dressed]

MENS' CLOTHING

A long-sleeved woollen vest, better known as a 'ganzie' was worn by most Black Country working-class men, along with a pair of long-legged underpants. Over these was worn a flannelette shirt, a moleskin waistcoat and corduroy or moleskin trousers tied at the knee with string, or narrow leather straps with buckles, and held up at the waist by a broad leather belt with a large buckle fastener. Heavy, hob-nailed boots or clogs, a muffler scarf, and a peaked cloth cap completed the outfit. Despite the obvious poverty, most people kept a 'Sunday best' outfit, often retrieved from

the pawnshop on Saturday evening and popped back in on Monday morning. For men it was a rather tight-fitting, sombre coloured, three piece suit, a shirt with heavily starched 'fly-away' collar, highly polished boots, and a 'billy-cock' bowler hat or cloth cap. Those men fortunate enough to sport a fob watch kept it in their waistcoat pocket with the attached chain secured to a buttonhole, and a flower in their coat buttonhole, was a common sight on Sundays.

Mens' Clothing
—By kind permission of Jim Harcourt

Group of Black Country quarry men in their 'Sunday best', enjoying a drink outside the Four Ways Public House, Portway Road, Rowley Regis, at the turn of the century.

WOMEN'S CLOTHING

Very drab clothing was worn by working-class women on week days. Long, black, full skirts made from alpacca cotton which rustled as they moved; a plain, high-necked, tight-bodiced blouse with leg-o-mutton

THE LATEST FASHIONS.

Now that the London milliners are flocking back from Paris, the new modes are being revealed to us one after the other. There is no diminution in the variety of bonnets and hats. Nearly every possible shape is worn, and our artist has illustrated three types among many, in the three figures we give this week. The first shows a hat of fancy straw, bordered with a narrow quilling of lace. The model from which it was sketched was trimmed with velvet-petalled roses in a deep tone of yellow, two of them being tucked under the brim at each side, on the top of the strings. The feathers are black, and the wing bows are of lace or chiffon. The beauty of the artificial flowers this season is quite beyond praise. The French excel in their manufacture, and the good ones are very costly. If our own workers were but

given technical training in their youth they might have some chance of equalling the French, but they seem to think it right to try one trade after another, wasting time and experience, and eventually stagger into flower-making in a kind of casual way. It is the same with embroiderers; and when one thinks of the thousands of pounds that are paid for these yearly, it does seem regrettable that at least a portion should not be earned by our own countrywomen. Exquisite embroideries are seen on some of the new hats and bonnets. The raised bullion work familiar to us on officers' uniforms is now applied to bonnets, and even the ecclesiastical embroideries are occasionally pressed into the service of beauty in this way.

Our second sketch shows a smart cape in violet cloth built in two storeys. The flat revers that finish

the fronts and form a collar is in heliotrope silk braided in gold. The two cords that fasten it across the front are in violet and gold. Some of the newest capes of this length measure five yards round the edge, and yet fall in much more closely to the figure than this one. The secret of this is that they are cut out of very wide cloth, on which the pattern is laid in a circle, the centre of which forms the neck of the cape when it is cut out. Skirts look as if they were cut in the same way, so closely do they fit about the hips and so wide are they about the feet. The hems are lined with stout linen which is very stiff indeed. This lining is preferable to horse-hair for some

reasons. The latter is apt to escape through the lining and assault the ankles, when shoes are worn instead of boots. It is most uncomfortable; but so is dress generally just at present, as well as very extravagant. Mirror velvets and shaded silks are extremely high in price. We saw a shaded mirror velvet the other day, the price of which per yard was nine guineas. The colours were lovely, it is true, shading from palest green to softest blue, grey, dove-colour, tender mauve, and faintest lemon. But most persons would find it beyond their purses, and might say:

> "If it be not fair for me,
> What care I how fair it be?"

The Midland Sun

SATURDAY, APRIL 15TH, 1893.

sleeves and over this an apron with large patch pockets. Often, another waist apron known as a [baggin appon] was worn, made from hurden [erden] cloth usually obtained from sugar bags. Underwear was in the main homemade and heavily starched but the most uncomfortable must surely have been the crocheted brassiere tied at the back, which some women painstakingly made. Their hair was worn long and after the age of eighteen was scooped up into a neat 'bun'. Hair nets made of chenille held these buns in place and were called 'snoods' but about this time it was fashionable for women to frizz their hair by thrusting curling tongs into the fire until hot and then twirling them around strands of their hair, often with disastrous results.

Womens' clothing — Typical 'best outfit' for working-class women at the turn of the century

A mixture of half a pint of boiling water, a piece of soap the size of a pea and one tablespoon of borax was used to dampen hair before frizzing, as this held the shape of the curl longer. Elastic-sided boots were worn but button-up boots were more popular, requiring a button hook to pull the buttons through the holes. Older women always wore shawls. Caps embroidered with tiny black beads and black bonnets with feathers on the side and ribbons tied under the chin were, however, worn by the better dressed women for Church or Chapel.

Button Hook

More elaborate and colourful dresses, invariably homemade were kept for Sundays but some older women could be seen clothed completely in black, wearing mens' peaked cloth caps and smoking clay pipes. When a death occurred it was customary for women to go into 'first mourning', for the first nine months when only black clothes were worn, followed by a further nine months in 'second mourning' when a less severe outfit was permitted together with jet and feather trimmings on bonnets. The next six months known as 'half mourning' permitted women to wear more jet trimmings, to remove veils on bonnets and to replace with mourning flowers or feathers. It was two years before colours could be worn and then only grey and purple gradually re-introduced, by which time another death had probably occurred in the family.

Reproduced from the Dudley Almanack

COSMETICS

Women throughout the ages have used cosmetics of a sort to enhance their appearance and Black Country women at the turn of the century were no exception. Make-up was very much frowned upon by the older generation but young women would secretly experiment with items such as flour or fine oatmeal as a substitute for face powder; red crepe paper dampened and the dye rubbed over cheeks as rouge; red cashou sweets for reddening lips; and even soot from the chimney to darken eyelashes and eyebrows. This was known as being 'painted up to the nines' but all traces of make-up had to be removed before father, the head of the family, returned home, otherwise they would have been branded as 'brazen hussies' [brairzon uzzies], and probably been given a [back-onda] as punishment.

CHILDRENS' CLOTHING

For the first six months, babies wore a piece of flannel called a 'binder' wrapped around their middle. Next to this was another flannel garment called a 'back flannel', then a long nightdress or dress and finally they were cocooned in a warm shawl. After six months, it was customary for the baby to be dressed in shorter clothes. This occasion was known as being 'shortened'.

Boy & girl on wall—by kind permission of Marilyn McDougall

Boys were often kept in dresses until they went to school, when their outfits changed to three-quarter length trousers with a band just below the knee, hand-knitted socks which fitted under the band, and a shirt with an uncomfortable detachable collar. These were heavily starched and often cut into the collar of the coats, so the discomfort of the wearer can well be imagined. A short, waist length jacket known as a 'bum freezer', and a peaked cloth cap completed the outfit. Socks were mainly hand-knitted and given a new lease of life when holes appeared; the worn out part on the foot was unpicked and re-footed with remnants of wool, irrespective of colour. When the socks were beyond repair the part below the heel was discarded leaving the upper section and the welt to be made into cosy mittens to wear during the

Typical Outfit for a little girl

By kind permission of Jim Harcourt

Jim as a boy dressed in his 'Sunday best'. Jim started work at the age of 13 and spent most of his working life in the Rowley quarries until his retirement

winter months. Cloths were patched and darned to give them a new lease of life and not until they were threadbare were they discarded or made into podged rugs.

Pinafores with deep frills edging the bottom and shoulders were worn by girls over their dresses. These pinafores also had large patch-pockets on either side referred to as [tay party pockets], so called because they were roomy enough for the wearer to take home for the rest of the family any left-over food from Sunday School or similar parties. Black stockings were worn over the knee and secured with one inch wide garters. Some girls were the proud possessors of glacé kid button-up shoes but many wore strong boots with heavy nails or studs in the soles, similar to those worn by boys. Girls always wore their long hair loosely and tied with ribbon, the girls with straight hair suffering the discomfort of having it wound up in 'rags' or twists of paper in order to have curls which were more fashionable at that time.

Beef Recipes

[Gerrit downya wazzin]

To save fuel, particularly in the summer months, it was not uncommon for women living in close proximity to a bakery to take their Sunday joint of meat to be cooked in the ovens alongside the bread, otherwise it was necessary to keep a huge fire roaring in the kitchen grate even in the hottest weather.

Beef was a popular, cheap Sunday roast in the early 1900's in the Black Country and was more accessible than poultry which was often only eaten at Christmas or for special occasions. Chine, sirloin and aitchbone were popular cuts and large joints were made to last for several meals. After Sunday dinner — always served at midday — it would be cut cold for supper and served with home-made pickles, beetroot or cold potatoes left from dinner. Monday was usually wash-day, so the remaining meat would be utilised in various ways. Hot Pot and Shepherds's Pie were favourites and easy to prepare but the following three recipes were other ways of using up the remains of the Sunday joint. These are followed by recipes for other cuts of beef, offal, and a savoury pudding.

NOVEMBER 5th 1900
Interesting Ceremony at the Dudley Corporation Electric Station, Springsmire. The Electric Light for the public streets switched on for the first time by Mrs G.H. Dunn.

Reproduced from the Dudley Almanack

HASH

Cold cooked beef
Carrots, onions, leeks, swede and parsnip
Diced potato
Salt and pepper

Mince the meat together with the vegetables and place in a saucepan with the diced potatoes, salt and pepper. Add the remainder of the cold gravy, supplemented with a little extra water or stock and simmer gently for about one hour. This was another simply prepared meal which could be left simmering gently on the hob while the family washing was being attended to.

COLD BEEF AND TOMATO PIE

4 sliced tomatoes
½ lb minced beef (remains of joint)
1 beaten egg
parsley
Salt and pepper
1 teacupful stock
Pastry

(Sufficient for two)

Grease a pie dish and layer with the meat, tomatoes, salt, pepper and parsley. Pour over the beaten egg and stock and cover with a pastry lid. Glaze with beaten egg or milk and bake for about one hour in a hot oven.

BEEF AND BREAD PUDDING

Approximately 1 lb cold cooked beef
8 oz sliced bread
Butter or dripping
1 large onion, chopped
1 teaspoon chopped parsley
1 teaspoon sage
Salt and pepper

(Sufficient for four)

Slice the meat thinly. Spread the slices of bread with butter or dripping. Line a two pint pudding basin with the bread, reserving some for the top. Layer the meat, onion, herbs and seasonings in the bread-lined basin and cover the top with the reserved slices. Cover the pudding basin with greased greaseproof paper, and cloth secured with string. Steam the pudding for about one hour. Serve with potatoes and any green vegetable.

As in many other areas of Britain, tripe was a very popular dish in the Black Country at the turn of the century and the following recipes are the two most practised methods.

TRIPE (Method 1)

Place bite-sized pieces of tripe, in a saucepan together with sliced onion, a little diced, cooked bacon, a little chopped parsley, milk to cover and salt and pepper to taste. Simmer gently for about one hour then thicken with flour or cornflour and water towards the end of the cooking time.

TRIPE (Method 2)

Fry pieces of tripe with onions in a little butter. Cover with milk, add a little chopped parsley, a bay leaf, salt and pepper and simmer for about one hour. Thicken with a little flour or cornflour and water.

COWHEEL AND BEEF PUDDING

1 lb shin of beef
1 onion stuck with cloves
1 cowheel
Salt and pepper
Suet crust

(Sufficient for four)

Cut the beef and cowheel into small pieces, add the onion, salt and pepper, cover with water, bring to the boil and simmer for about three hours. Strain and keep the liquid. Remove the bones and onion and mince the meat. Line a two pint basin with suet crust, add the meat, moisten with liquid and cover with a pastry lid. Steam for three hours. Make gravy with the remaining liquid and serve with mashed swede and potatoes.

POTTED BEEF'S CHEEK

1 Beef's cheek
1 lb shin of beef
1 large onion
Salt and pepper
A bay leaf

Thoroughly clean the beef's cheek and then boil all the ingredients for about three hours. Leave to cool in the liquid. Discard any fat or gristle and chop or mince the remainder roughly. Mix thoroughly and put the mixture into a basin. Add about six tablespoons of the juices, cover with a saucer and place a weight on the top to compress the meat mixture. Leave for several hours in a cool place and when completely set, invert on to a plate. This dish is especially tasty served with Sweet Beetroot Pickle.

BEEF AND EGG ROAST

2 lbs minced beef
3 eggs
½ lb suet
1 cup fresh breadcrumbs
Salt and pepper
Thyme and parsley
A dash of Worcestershire Sauce

(Sufficient for four)

Mix all the ingredients well together. Turn out on to a floured board, form into a roll or square and bake for one hour, basting well.

SAVOURY TOAST

Any surplus fat left from the Sunday joint of beef after the majority had been rendered down into dripping was cut into very small cubes, dotted over a round of bread and toasted until all the dripping had oozed from the fat and the fat itself was nice and crisp. Salt and pepper transformed this humble recipe into a satisfying and economical snack.

OXTAIL MOULD

1 Oxtail
2 hard-boiled eggs
Salt and pepper
Stock from oxtail

Cover the oxtail in water and stew for about two hours until tender. Remove the bones and surplus fat and add salt and pepper. Place a layer of sliced egg on the base of a small mould, cover with the oxtail and spoon a little of the stock over. Cover with a plate weighted down and leave until cold. Invert on to a plate to serve.

POTTED BEEF PASTE

2 lbs shin of beef
1 teaspoon salt
½ teaspoon pepper
4 teaspoons clarified butter

Cut the meat into very small pieces, season and place in a stone jar or basin. Cover with greased paper and stand the basin in a pan of water. Cover the pan and simmer for two hours. Strain the liquid into a bowl and add three ounces of the butter. Mince the meat several times until very smooth and mix with the liquid. Put into a clean jar or bowl and pour over it the remaining melted clarified butter. Keep in a cool place and use within two days.

BEEF ROLL

12 oz stewing steak
8 oz ham
4 oz fresh breadcrumbs
1 egg
Salt and pepper
Pinch of ground mace

Mince the beef and ham and combine with the remaining ingredients. Mix well and put into a greased two pound stone jam jar or similar modern container. Steam for about two hours.

POTTED MEAT (Method 1)

1 lb Rump steak
½ lb Ham
¼ lb breadcrumbs
2 eggs
Salt and pepper

Mince the steak and ham, add the breadcrumbs, salt and pepper and bind all together with the beaten eggs. Pile into a basin and steam for about two hours. Chill before serving.

POTTED MEAT (Method 2)

2 pig's feet
1 lb Shin of beef
1 teaspoon pickling spice
Salt and pepper
Water to cover

Boil all the ingredients together for about two hours. Remove the bones, mix well and place in a basin with a little of the juices poured over. Place a saucer and a weight on top to compress and leave until cold before inverting on to a plate.

KETTLE SOUP

Kettle Soup was the name chosen for a form of soup made with just a lump of beef dripping placed in a basin with hot water from the kettle poured over, the dripping often being the only remaining ingredient in the pantry. Served this way, it made a change from just bread spread with cold dripping and was the next best thing to a hot meal.

MARCH 1894
28—Fatal Accident to George Wise (15) on the Tram Line at Sedgley.

Reproduced from the Dudley Almanack

The following recipe was the Black Country equivalent of Yorkshire Pudding. It was a good 'filler', but often there was not enough room in the oven to cook it as a separate dish so this method evolved.

SEASONING PUDDING

6 oz stale bread
2 oz fine oatmeal
2 oz suet
3 eggs
½ pint hot milk
Pinch ceyenne pepper
Salt and pepper
1 teaspoon sage
1 teaspoon dripping

Soak the bread in the milk and put on one side to cool. Mix the dry ingredients into the bread mixture and bind with the beaten eggs. Remove the joint of meat from the oven about half an hour before it is cooked and pour most of the dripping into a container for use later. Spread the mixture over the remaining dripping in the base of the baking tin, replace the meat back on top and bake for about half an hour.

Last Monday the inhabitants of Oldbury were thrown into a state of considerable excitement by the sight of a tram running along the lines between West Bromwich and Oldbury. These trams come and go with quite surprising irregularity, and the company which owns them seem to be guided by a wisdom which we duller mortals cannot fathom. It is about three or four months ago now since they first began to cease running every day. Apparently, Monday seemed to be the day selected by them for appearing once again in a sudden blaze of glory; but lately even Monday has gone by without a tram being visible. Most of us, so Naturalists and other enemies of mankind say, resemble some animal of the lower kingdom. The Tram Company seems, on the whole, to bear a resemblance to a dormouse, whose habits of sleep are too well known to be recapitulated. The company satisfies its passion for work by dispatching one tram every week or fortnight from Oldbury to West Bromwich, and after that relapses into a quiet slumber till its demon of energy is again roused, and another tram is sent on its journey. The passenger traffic between the two places, in the morning and evening at any rate, is by no means a light one, and human nature would be quite satisfied with one or two trams running regularly throughout the week at those periods of the day.

From 'The Midland Sun' April 15th 1893

Lamb and Mutton Recipes

New season lamb in the spring and early summer was merely complimented with the first of the home-grown new potatoes, fresh peas and mint sauce. No other variations were considered necessary. Mutton, however, was eaten regularly throughout the winter months, as the cheaper cuts such as neck and breast involved little preparation and a complete meal for the entire family could be left simmering all morning in a huge stewpot on a hob at the side of the fire. Swedes, carrots, onions, leeks, pearl barley and dumplings were added and the meal often served with onion sauce, caper sauce, or parsley sauce. The recipes which follow, however, were welcome alternatives in some households.

STEAMED MUTTON AND RICE

Neck of mutton
1 teacup rice
1 large onion
1 lb carrots
1 small swede
Butter for frying

(Sufficient for four)

Trim the excess fat from a neck of mutton and cut the meat into small chops. Place in a saucepan together with a teacup of rice and a little salt and pepper. Gently fry the sliced onion, carrot and swede and add to the meat. Cover with water and leave to simmer gently for about two hours. Serve with boiled potatoes.

STEAMED MUTTON

Place bite-size pieces of mutton in a greased pudding basin with a little water, salt and pepper. Cover with a buttered paper and steam for three hours with the lid of the saucepan fitting tightly. When cooked, add a tablespoon of Worcestershire Sauce to the gravy and serve the dish with potatoes and a green vegetable.

MINCED LAMB/MUTTON TOASTIES

The following snack is made from left-over lamb or mutton. The meat is first minced and sprinkled with a little flour, salt and pepper and a dusting of nutmeg. A small chopped onion is fried until soft in a little butter and the meat mixture added together with sufficient stock or gravy to cover. This is simmered gently for about half an hour when it is served on toast or fried bread.

STUFFED LAMB'S LIVER

1 lb lamb's liver (unsliced)
1 lb onions (boiled in salted water until soft)
1 cup fresh breadcrumbs
2 tablespoons fresh sage or
1 tablespoon dried sage
1 heaped tablespoon plain flour

(Sufficient for four)

Wash and dry the liver and make a few gashes through. Make a stuffing by combining the onions, breadcrumbs and sage. Fill the gashes in the liver with the stuffing and carefully fry the underside in dripping, basting frequently until the liver is cooked. Cover with water and bake in a slow oven for about one hour. Thicken with flour and water, return to the oven and continue baking for a further 30 minutes. Serve with mashed potato and a green vegetable.

JULY 1895

17—Election Fracas at Tipton. William Wassell seriously injured.
30—Death of William Wassell . . . at the Guest Hospital.

Reproduced from the Dudley Almanack

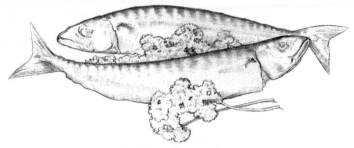

Fish Recipes

[Smosh tha boons wi viniga]

The popular choice of white fish such as cod, hake, or halibut was usually boiled, steamed or baked and served with potatoes and parsley sauce, as this required little attention. Herrings and mackerel were also popular as they were comparatively cheap and were fried over an open fire and eaten with just bread and butter. Fish rissoles helped to make a small amount of fish go a long way but the following recipes show a little more imagination.

BOILED HERRINGS

Clean the fish and remove the eyes. Put the tail through the eyeholes and boil them gently for about half an hour in water to which half a teacupful of vinegar has been added. Serve with bread and butter.

HERRINGS AND ONIONS

Slice and fry the onions in a little fat and fry the herrings until browned. Serve together piping hot with bread and butter.

FISH STEWED IN A JAR

Place one pound of white fish in an earthenware jar with a small knob of butter and a clove. Cover with a plate and place in a saucepan of boiling water. Keep the water steadily boiling for about half an hour. Serve with mustard or parsley sauce and vegetables, or just bread and butter.

FISH AND LEEK BAKE

4 cod steaks
2 lbs leeks
1 onion
1 lemon
Salt and pepper
2 oz butter
Parsley

(Sufficient for four)

Fish Kettle,
with drainer and cover

Clean and slice the leeks and onion and fry gently in a little butter or oil or combination of both, for a few minutes. Line the bottom of a dish with the leeks and onions and place the cod steaks on top. Season with salt and pepper and sprinkle with the juice of a lemon and a little parsley. Dot with butter, cover with greased paper and bake for about one hour in a medium oven. Serve with chips or mashed potato.

COD'S HEAD AND SHOULDERS

1 Cod's head and shoulders
4 oz of salt to each gallon water
3 tablespoons of vinegar
A little horseradish

(Sufficient for two)

Lay the fish in a fish kettle or shallow pan with sufficient salted water to cover it. Add the vinegar and horseradish, bring to the boil and simmer gently until the fish is cooked. Remove the fish from the bones and serve with potato and parsley sauce. Cod's heads were very cheap and were often given away, so lots of women made full use of this opportunity, providing a substantial meal for their families.

PICKLED SALMON

Cut a salmon into slices and poach gently for about ten minutes. Take a pint of the liquor in which the salmon was boiled and add half an ounce of whole black peppers, a quarter of an ounce of allspice and boil for

79

about fifteen minutes. Lay the salmon into a deep dish and pour the pickle liquid over it. Add a little salad oil and ceyenne pepper and cover it closely. It will keep indefinitely.

BLACK COUNTRY FISH PIE

The fish from 2 Cod's heads and shoulders
(previously boiled)
Equivalent weight in mashed potatoes and parsnips
A little melted butter
A little cayenne
1 hard-boiled egg

(Sufficient for four)

Grease a pie dish and fill with layers of flaked fish and potatoes and parsnips. Sprinkle with cayenne and bake for about twenty minutes in a medium oven. Turn out on to a plate and garnish with the sliced egg and a little melted butter or sauce of one's choice

BAKED HAKE

Hake left in one piece but head removed
Homemade thyme and parsley stuffing
Egg and breadcrumbs

(Sufficient for four)

Gut and clean the fish thoroughly and fill with the stuffing. Bake in a medium oven until the fish parts easily from the bones. Serve with chipped potatoes.

BAKED EELS

4 large eels
A little clear stock
A bunch of savoury herbs
A sprig of parsley
2 glasses of elderberry or port wine
The juice of a small lemon
Salt and Cayenne
1 teaspoon Worcestershire sauce

(Sufficient for four)

Skin and clean the eels and divide into small pieces. Wipe them dry, dip each piece into a seasoning of cayenne, salt, minced parsley, and a little chopped herbs. Place them in a deep dish, cover them with the stock, place a greased paper over and bake until the eels are tender. Skim off the fat and remove the fish to a hot dish to keep warm. Stir into the gravy the wine, strained lemon juice, and sauce. Bring to the boil and pour over the fish. Garnish with sliced lemon.

BAKED PIKE

A large pike (head removed)
A quantity of homemade thyme and parsley stuffing
A little butter
The peel of a lemon
1 glass of elderberry or port wine
1 tablespoon of Worcestershire sauce
One teaspoon of capers

(Sufficient for four to six)

Gut and clean the pike thoroughly and fill with the stuffing, securing with thread or skewers. Place in a large baking dish and sprinkle with salt. Dot with butter and bake in a moderate oven for about one hour. Remove carefully on to a dish to keep warm and make a sauce from the remaining ingredients, thickened with a little flour and water. Serve the sauce separately.

Reproduced from the Dudley Almanack

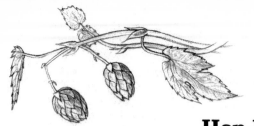

Hop-Picking

[Gooin down th'op Country]

Holidays were out of the question for most Black Country families, the majority never seeing the sea at all during their lifetime. A visit to the surrounding countryside or nearest riverside was considered a rare treat but every summer there was a mass exodus of families to the hopyards of Hereford, Newnham Bridge, Pershore, Holt Fleet, Tenbury and Bromyard, where the women and children stayed for several weeks helping to harvest the crops. This was known as [gooin down th'op country]. It was just another means of earning extra money but the change of scene served as a holiday and although the living conditions left a lot to be desired, a good time was generally had by all. Parents often neglected to obtain permission of leave from school for their children which created great problems to the Education Authorities.

The trips were organised by women known as 'Hirers' who for their part received a commission from the overseer. Return fares for each

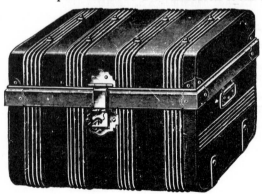

Hopping Box

family were paid for by the farmer. Eager families lined the railway stations where special trains with extra carriages were standing ready to transport hop-pickers to the hopyards and because of their extreme length, gave rise to the Black Country expression "as long as a hop-picking train". As the carriages filled, the Station Master's cry of "Hop Pickers only" could be heard above the excited chatter of the families. Clothes and possessions [tranklements] were packed into tea chests and tin trunks known as 'hopping boxes', which proved useful both for transporting clothes and personal belongings to the hopyards and for bringing home a supply of fruit on the return journey. On arrival, waggons or carts drawn by shire-horses collected the hop-pickers' belongings from the station with the hop-pickers themselves following on foot.

With the exception of the 'lady hop-picker', all the hop-picking photos are by kind permission of Jim Aldridge. The preacher touring the hopyards with his caravan was his Grandfather

The living accommodation was very primitive, usually empty lambing or cow sheds, but despite the cramped communal living quarters and far from adequate amenities, everyone made the most of the situation. Nothing else was expected and families were allocated their own section of the sheds to make as comfortable as they could. Bales of straw were provided for bedding, each family making one enormous bed about one foot deep, compressed down and covered with their own blankets. It was considered a joke amongst themselves that these beds only became comfortable when it was time to return home. To seclude themselves away from other families, the trunks and tea chests were placed at the end of their beds and blankets haphazardly strung around, creating a little more privacy. The sheds were lit by oil lamps

hung on hooks and the only indoor toilet facilities during the night were buckets lined with straw "to muffle the sound". To add to the discomfort, rats often scurried amongst the rafters.

Meals were cooked mainly in the open on a mammoth fire built close to the living quarters. Simple dishes were prepared but some women took along with them enamel saucepans with three different sections similar to a steamer, and were able to cook a variety of food at one time. The fresh air and exercise generated tremendous appetites so lots of filling dishes were prepared but sandwiches were the mainstay, together with copious amounts of strong tea [stewed tay] drunk from enamel mugs. Wooden trestles were a substitute for tables, and newspapers replaced tablecloths. Picking hops was tiring work and a rough and ready attitude was considered part and parcel of the outdoor life.

3 Part Steamer

The hop vines were trained to grow up and over three wires stretched from creosoted posts; the first wire about six inches from the ground, the second about six feet and the third along the top of the posts which were about eighteen feet high. String was attached from wire to wire enabling the vines to cling. A section of the hopfield was allocated to each family and these areas were known as 'houses'.

Hooks attached to long poles were used to pull the vines down from the netting, enabling the family to pick the hops which were then thrown into a 'crib', a container made from wooden supports with a hessian sack slung inside, care being taken to avoid the inclusion of leaves. A man known as a 'Busheller' periodically toured the site collecting and measuring hops into a wicker basket which, as the name implies held approximately one bushel, but these Bushellers were notoriously renowned for compressing the hops down in the basket, making the

Lady hop-picker—B.C.M.
The crib can be seen in the background

weight good, much to the annoyance of the pickers. The crop of hops were then taken to the kilns and spaced out on a slatted floor over a stove or furnace. The heat was evenly distributed by draughts below and around them and the hops took about ten hours to dry before being removed from the kiln, allowed to cool and then stored.

Work started early in the morning and continued through 'till dusk with just a break at midday. Fingers became badly stained with continual hop-picking and left a very bitter, disagreeable taste if hands were not washed before eating food but this was soon adjusted to, along with the pungent, heady smell of the hops. Most evenings, families made their way to the nearest pub to relax with a drink, singsong and a chat and weekends in particular were eagerly awaited, for this was when relatives, unable to accompany the hop-pickers on their holiday because of work commitments, visited the hop yards bringing with them extra supplies of food and money.

It was common practise to have a 'sub' from the overseer at the beginning of the week and some pickers had very little money due to them on payday after settling their debts. More prudent families, however, made the most of the opportunity to earn a little extra money. Traders visited hopyards with food, the most popular with the children

being the 'Lardy Cake Man' selling his cakes from a basket. Preachers were also known to visit the hopyards and usually arrived by horse-drawn caravan, frequently to be met with such derisive remarks as "What time does the circus start?"

Living in such close proximity to each other obviously created problems and occasionally a brawl would erupt but in general there was a community spirit and people helped each other when difficulties arose. The fresh air and open spaces proved beneficial and after lining the bottom of their tin trunks with apples, sometimes purchased legitimately from the farmer, but more often than not, 'scrumped', the families made their way homeward as brown as berries, often 'lousey' but ready to face the oncoming winter.

Puddings

[Fill Bally]

All the well-known filling dishes such as Apple Pie, Roly Poly Pudding, Plum Duff and Steamed Treacle Pudding were enjoyed with relish in the Black Country but most of the following recipes are more exclusive to this area and were especially popular with mothers of large families as they were both filling and economical.

TREACLE CUSTARD

Shortcrust pastry
2 eggs
4 tablespoons syrup
Rind and juice of 2 lemons

Grease and line a deep plate with pastry. Beat the egg and warmed syrup together and add the lemon rind and juice. Pour the mixture into a pastry-lined plate and bake in a slow oven until golden brown. Eat cold, when the mixture will have set like a jelly.

MIXED MEDLEY

Mixture of fresh fruit i.e. strawberries, raspberries, cherries, sliced apple, sliced banana, red and black currants, bilberries, rhubarb, plums, damsons, or any fruit in season
Sugar to taste

Bake all the ingredients except the banana together in a slow oven for about one hour. Leave until cold before adding the sliced banana. This dish was usually served with custard but fresh cream was an alternate luxury.

BARLEY AND APPLE PUDDING

½ lb pearl barley
2 large cooking apples (stewed with 2 oz sugar)
pinch of cinnamon

Wash the pearl barley and soak it in water overnight. Place it in a pan with three pints of water and let it boil for two hours. Drain and mix thoroughly with stewed apple and cinnamon. Place in a buttered pie dish and bake in a moderate oven for about one hour.

BANANA CUSTARD

3 ripe bananas
3 beaten eggs
2 teaspoons sugar
Vanilla essence
Lemon essence
1 pt milk
Knob of butter

Mash the bananas to a pulp and add the beaten eggs, sugar and a few drops of vanilla and lemon essence. Stir in one pint of milk and pour into a buttered pie dish. Dot with a few pieces of butter and bake in a moderate oven for about one hour.

CRUNCHY APPLE CHARLOTTE

Bread (broken into bite-size pieces)
Cooking apples (sliced)
Sugar
Suet
Butter or margarine

Grease a pie dish and place alternate layers of bread, apples, and a sprinkling of suet and sugar ending with a layer of bread. Sprinkle with a little sugar and dot with butter. Bake in a moderate oven until the top layer of bread is crunchy and the sides and bottom, sticky and toffee-like.

MILK DUMPLINGS

3 oz flour
2 oz sugar
Pinch of salt
2 oz dripping
1 fl oz water

SAUCE

1 pint of milk
2 oz sugar
Juice of a lemon
1 oz cornflour

Bring the water to the boil and melt the dripping in it. Mix gradually the dry ingredients with the water and make about nine small dumplings. Roll them in a little extra flour and simmer for about seven minutes in the milk, stirring gently with a fork. They are ready when they rise to the top of the milk. After removing the dumplings to keep warm, bring the milk to boiling point, thicken with the cornflour mixed with a little water and add the sugar and lemon juice. Pour the sauce over the dumplings and serve at once.

BLACKBERRY AND BULLACE PUDDING

½ lb blackberries
½ lb damsons or plums (the original recipe called for bullaces
which are a variety of wild fruit resembling damsons, but yellow
in colour and very bitter)
Sugar to sweeten the fruit
Slices of bread

Line a greased pie-dish with slices of bread and gently stew the black-berries and plums together with the sugar. Put layers of the fruit mixture and bread into the dish, ending with a layer of bread and let the dish stand overnight. Invert on to a plate and serve with custard or cream.

Bullaces, mentioned above were also substituted for apples in jams and preserves requiring more pectin as they gave a better setting quality.

BLACKBERRY & DAMSON PUDDING

½ lb damsons
½ lb blackberries
About 3 oz sugar
2 oz plain flour
1 egg
½ pt milk

Stew the blackberries and damsons together with the sugar and make a batter with the flour, egg and milk. Grease the outside of a pound stone jar and place it in a greased tin or pie dish allowing enough room to pour the batter into. Bake in a hot oven until set. Remove the jar and fill the remaining cavity with the fruit mixture. Serve with custard or cream. (Today, a savarin mould would be substituted for the jar and dish method above).

APPLE AND TREACLE TART

½ lb shortcrust pastry
1 lb cooking apples
2 tablespoons golden syrup
1 cup fresh breadcrumbs
A little grated nutmeg

Line a greased pie dish with the pastry and cover with a layer of peeled, cored and chopped apples. Warm the syrup and pour over the apples. Sprinkle with breadcrumbs and nutmeg and cover with a pastry lid. Bake in a moderate oven for about half an hour. Serve with custard or cream.

APPLE AND LEMON PUDDING

6 cooking apples
¼ lb butter
2 eggs
3 oz sugar
Juice and grated rind of a lemon
Breadcrumbs

Stew the apples and sugar and add the butter. When cold, add the beaten eggs, lemon juice and rind. Butter a pie dish and cover the bottom and sides thickly with crumbs. Pour in the apple mixture and cover with more crumbs, dot with butter and bake until brown in a moderate oven.

FIVE MINUTE PUDDING

3 tablespoons flour
3 dessertspoons sugar
1 dessertspoon baking powder
2 eggs
A little jam

Mix all the ingredients together except the jam. Spread the mixture on to an oblong baking tin and bake for five minutes in a moderate oven. Spread with a thin layer of jam and form into a roll. Serve with custard.

GROUND RICE PUDDING

¼ lb ground rice
¼ lb flour
¼ lb suet
2 oz brown sugar
1 teacup raisins (chopped)
1 level teaspoon bicarbonate of soda
1 large teacup milk
Pinch of salt

Mix all the dry ingredients together and then add the milk. Pile into a buttered pie dish and boil or steam for three hours.

AUNT LOUISA'S PUDDING

1 pint of breadcrumbs
2 pints of milk
6 oz sugar
2 oz butter
Peel and juice of one lemon
5 eggs
Apricot Jam

Pour 1½ pints of the warm milk over the bread and mix well together. Add the remaining milk, grated lemon rind, 3 oz sugar, butter and the yolks of the eggs. Beat well together, pour into a dish and bake in a medium oven for about thirty minutes. Whisk the egg whites until stiff and then add the lemon juice with the remaining sugar. Cover the top of the pudding with a thick layer of apricot jam, spread the whisked egg whites over the top, return to the oven and cook until the top is nicely browned.

POTATO PUDDING

1 lb potatoes
½ lb sugar
½ lb butter
5 eggs
Peel and juice of a lemon

Boil the potatoes until tender then press through a sieve. Cream the butter and sugar together until light and fluffy, mix with the potatoes and add all the remaining ingredients. Mix together thoroughly, place in greased pie-dish and bake in a hot oven for about thirty minutes.

CAKE FRITTERS

Cut a stale cake into slices about an inch and a half in thickness. Pour a little milk over each slice and fry them gently in a little butter. When done, spread with a layer of jam.

RUSSET APPLE PUDDING

8 Russet Apples
Yolks of 3 eggs
3 oz butter
Short Crust pastry
Grated rind of a lemon

Peel and core the apples and boil them to a pulp with the lemon peel. Beat the egg yolks with the softened butter, sweeten to taste and beat all well together. Line a pie dish with the pastry and pour in the mixture. Bake in a moderate oven until lightly browned.

APPLE CUSTARD PUDDING

3 large cooking apples
Grated rind of one lemon
1 pint of milk
2 oz sugar
4 well beaten eggs

Peel, core and slice the apples and stew gently until tender. Add the lemon rind and mix well. Pour into a pie dish and leave to cool. Make a custard with the milk, sugar, and eggs and pour over the apple mixture. Bake in a moderate oven for about thirty minutes.

FUN PUDDING

Short Crust pastry
Raspberry or Strawberry Jam
Sponge fingers (or stale sponge cake)
½ pint milk
1 oz butter
1 dessertspoon flour
Grated peel of 1 lemon
2 eggs
A little sugar
A trace of nutmeg

Line a greased pie dish with the pastry. Put a layer of jam on top, followed by a layer of sponge fingers. Make a sauce with the milk, butter and flour. Add the grated lemon rind and when cold, add the egg yolks, nutmeg and sugar to taste. Pour over the sponge fingers and bake in a moderate oven for about half an hour. Whisk the egg whites until stiff and cover the top of the pudding when baked. Return it to the oven for a few minutes until nicely browned.

HASTY PUDDING

½ pint boiling milk
1 egg
1 heaped tablespoon flour
A little salt
½ teacup of cold milk
Sugar to taste

Make a batter with the egg, flour, salt and cold milk. Pour into the boiling milk add the sugar and stir until it is cooked.

SIPPET PUDDING

Thin slices of bread
Shredded suet
Currants
2 eggs
1 pint milk
2 oz sugar
Grated nutmeg

Place a layer of bread in the bottom of a well-greased baking dish and sprinkle the bread with suet and currants. Continue in layers until the dish is three parts full. Beat together the eggs, milk, sugar, and nutmeg and pour over the bread. Bake in a moderate oven until the custard is set and the top nicely browned.

STRAWBERRY PUDDING

Fresh breadcrumbs
Washed and hulled strawberries
Sugar
Shredded suet
A little butter

Grease a baking dish and fill with alternate layers of bread crumbs, strawberries, sugar and shredded suet, ending with bread crumbs. Dot with butter and bake in a medium oven for about one hour.

BLACKBERRY PUDDING

1 lb blackberries
3 oz sugar
Thin slices of bread
A little milk
Knob of butter

Mix the blackberries with the sugar. Place in a pie dish with alternate layers of the bread moistened with a little milk, ending with a layer of bread. Dot with butter and a sprinkling of sugar and bake in a hot oven for about half an hour. Any other soft fruits can be substituted for the blackberries.

RICE PUDDING WITH MARMALADE

1 teacup of short grain rice
2 cups of milk
2 oz sugar
1 tablespoon orange marmalade
1 egg

Boil the rice in a pint of water for ten minutes. Add the milk and simmer for half an hour without stirring. Add the sugar, marmalade and the well-beaten egg. Mix well together, pour into a pudding dish and bake in a medium oven for one hour.

POTATO PASTRY

4 oz flour
3 oz mashed potatoes
2 oz lard
Cold water
¼ teaspoon baking powder
¼ teaspoon salt

Sieve the salt and baking powder into the flour, rub in the lard, add the mashed potatoes and mix in lightly with cold water to a stiff dough. Use for either savoury pies or fruit pies and tarts.

STEAMED CARROT PUDDING

4 oz grated carrot
4 oz flour
3 oz breadcrumbs
1 egg
1 teaspoon baking powder
¼ pint milk
1 oz sugar
6 oz dried fruit
2 oz shredded suet

Mix the dry ingredients together with the grated carrot. Add milk to make a fairly dry mixture. Turn into a greased basin, cover with greased paper and steam for about 2 hours.

CHOCOLATE APPLE PUDDING

6 oz flour
1 teaspoon baking powder
2 oz margarine
3 oz golden syrup
1½ oz cocoa
1 large cooking apple
A little milk

Sieve the baking powder into the flour and rub in the margarine. Add the syrup and cocoa. Peel and chop the apple and with the other ingredients mix with the milk to give a soft dough. Steam in a greased basin for about 1½ hours. Serve with a thin custard sauce.

DATE AND APPLE PIE

Shortcrust pastry
½ lb dates (stoned)
1 lb cooking apples

Wash the dates, put them into a basin, cover with boiling water and soak for 1 hour. Strain, then chop the dates and core and slice the apples. Fill a pie-dish, cover with pastry and bake in a moderately hot oven for about 45 minutes.

BAKED FIG ROLL

Potato Pastry (page 97)
½ lb dried figs
A little nutmeg
Boiling water

Chop the figs and put them into a basin, cover with boiling water. Allow to stand for about twenty minutes, then pour off the water. Add the nutmeg and mash with a fork. Prepare the pastry and roll into an oblong. Moisten the edges and spread the fig filling to within an inch of the edge. Roll up and secure the ends. Bake on a greased baking sheet in a hot oven for about 45 minutes. Serve with custard.

ELDERBERRY AND APPLE PIE

½ lb shortcrust pastry
1 lb cooking apples, peeled, cored and stewed
1 lb elderberries
Sugar to sweeten
Rind of an orange

Grease a pie dish and cover with two thirds of the pastry, reserving the remainder for the lid. Combine the elderberries with the stewed apple, sugar and orange rind, and pile into the dish. Cover with the pastry lid and bake in a hot oven for about twenty minutes.

INVALID EGG JELLY

¾ oz gelatine
2 lemons
1 small teacup of sugar
2 eggs

Dissolve the gelatine in one gill of cold water, add the rind of the lemons and let it stand for one hour. Add one gill of boiling water, the sugar, the juice of the lemons and the beaten eggs. Stir well together and simmer gently in a saucepan for about fifteen minutes. Sieve, pour into a mould and leave until set.

VELVET CREAM

¼ oz gelatine
½ pint milk + 2 tablespoons
2 oz sugar
1 egg yolk
A little jam
Flavouring

Soak the gelatine in enough milk to cover it. When soft, pour over half a pint of boiling milk, the sugar and a flavouring of one's choice. Stir until dissolved. Let it cool, add the yolk of an egg and beat all well together. Line the bottom of a dish with jam and when the cream is nearly set, pour it slowly over the jam and leave until cold.

Schooling

[Learnin ta spake proppa]

In the early 1900's many children started school at three years of age and left at thirteen or even earlier. Basic lessons were known as the three R's — reading, writing and arithmetic but older girls learned to sew, knit, darn, crochet, launder and cook. Boys practised woodwork. Children commenced in Standard One and if the yearly exams were passed satisfactorily, would advance one grade until they had graduated to Standard Seven, the highest grade. Very few working-class children were privileged enough to have higher education. To mark the occasion of leaving, it was customary for children to receive a prize in the form of a book with an inscription inside of the child's name and the date of presentation.

Female teachers dressed very somberly in long black skirts and white blouses with whale-bone supports at the neck which gave an air of authority. Discipline was very severe in all schools, canes being displayed in a prominent position as a warning. Girls and boys alike were severely disciplined at home as well as at school and thought twice about doing anything out of step, knowing full well that punishment would be administered from one source or another, frequently both. It was not uncommon for fathers to remove their leather belts and beat their wayward sons to punish them, often for a trivial offence, and caning in schools was an everyday occurrence. The majority of children, however, were hardy and if a child was of a particularly rebellious nature, he was known as a [rantall].

It was a constant problem for mothers with large families to keep their childrens' hair free from lice. To combat this, fine toothcombs

Pupils of the Knowle School, Springfield, Rowley Regis, in the early 1900's. The teacher was the author's aunt

were used daily and a special brand of soap called 'Derbac' was used for washing hair. In extreme cases, vinegar or even paraffin was rubbed into the hair and scalp before washing to rid them of these head lice. A special Health Nurse regularly toured the schools to check on the state of childrens' hair. She was a dreaded visitor and was commonly called [the nuss oo looks ya'red] or just [th'nit nuss]. Children severely infested with head lice were sent home to get their hair cleared but it was a never ending problem.

The Sabbath was strictly observed by most families, with members attending Sunday School, Church or Chapel several times during the day. It was considered very disrespectful and even bad luck to sing anything but hymns on Sundays and children were reprimanded if they were caught singing or whistling a tune. In the summer, garden parties were arranged for the children in the grounds of the vicarage where tea was provided in paper bags containing a bread roll, a slice of cake, an apple, sweets and occasionally there would be a new penny amongst the delights. After tea, games were played and races run in the adjoining fields. Another special occasion for the children was the yearly anniversary of the Church or Chapel, when they assembled in

'Anniversary' photo — By kind permission of Clarry Siviter, whose father, John Edward was Sunday School Superintendent of the Cradley Heath and District Band of Hope Union. Every Whitsuntide a concert and competition was held at the Whitley Memorial School, Cradley Heath, where local Sunday Schools competed for the coveted 'banner' prize. The banner was then paraded round the surrounding streets with the children following on foot. Should the banner be won by the same group for three successive years, it was then handed over to them. These processions have long since been discontinued and the banner was donated to the Black Country Museum in recent years

the choir stalls or on a platform dressed in their Sunday best to give their rendering of childrens' hymns and recitations of heart-rending poems like the following:

> Only a drop in the bucket but every drop will tell.
> The bucket would soon be empty without the drops in the well.
> Only a poor little penny, it was all I had to give,
> But as pennies make the shillings, it may help some cause to live.
> God loveth the cheerful giver, though the gift be great or small,
> But what would he think of his children who never give at all.

The Anniversary was often followed by a parade of the children carrying banners through the streets to the accompaniment of a brass band whilst collections for the church funds were being made from door to door. Sometimes the children rode around the streets on a

Edwardian children in classroom (1910) —Dudley Reference Library

decorated 'float;' (a flat, horse-drawn waggon), waving flags and singing hymns. A prize in the form of a book inscribed with the child's name was given on these occasions for good attendance throughout the year.

Trips on horse-drawn brakes into the nearby countryside were arranged for the summer months along with trips on the canals when excited children, resplendent in their 'Sunday Best' and with wonderment in their eyes, stepped aboard canal boats specially cleaned, decorated and fitted out with benches from the Church or Chapel and on pushing away from the side of the canal, squealed with delight as they all sang in unison a popular hymn of the day "We are out on the ocean sailing".

Possibly more enjoyment was had on these occasions than children today have holidaying abroad, treats then being few and far between and each one greatly appreciated and enjoyed to the full.

Canal outing — By kind permission of Gayner Iddles.

Sunday School outing on the canal for children attending Toll End Weslyan Chapel in Aston Street, Tipton, known locally as 'Toll End Wesley'. Gayner's Grandfather, Father and several aunts are featured in the photograph. Her grandfather was the Superintendent and caretaker of the Sunday School. The family lived in a very humble dwelling attached to the Chapel, rent free and free coal as a bonus. As a consequence, there was always a roaring fire in the grate and visitors on Sundays could join in the services of the Chapel which penetrated the adjoining walls, without actually going to Chapel!

RED CROSS-STREET CHURCH OF ENGLAND SUNDAY SCHOOLS.

On Thursday last the children attending these Sunday Schools had their annual excursion. They were accompanied by their teachers and a number of parents and friends, the party numbering altogether nearly 300. The place chosen was Ellowes Hall, Ruiton, the seat of John L. Gibbons, Esq., one of the most delightful spots in the Black Country. The brakes, ten in number, were supplied by Mr. H. Careless. A start was made from Red Cross-street, Wolverhampton, at 2.30. The charming weather, which left nothing to be desired, contributed in no small degree to the afternoon's enjoyment. On arriving at Ruiton the party assembled in front of the hall, and sang the hymn "Children of the Heavenly King," after which all proceeded to the beautiful and extensive park adjoining, which afforded ample room for the enjoyment of football, cricket, rounders, see-saw, and other games. An excellent tea was provided, which being served under the canopy of Heaven and amid such beautiful surroundings, was heartily appreciated by all. After tea the teachers and friends were photographed by Mr. Bennett Clark. By the courtesy of Mr. and Mrs.

Gibbons the adults were permitted to walk through the garden and conservatories, the children meantime competing in various contests for prizes. As the shades of evening began to fall, the children again assembled in front of the hall and sang "God be with you till we meet again," after which Mr. John O. Lee, in felicitous terms, thanked Mr. and Mrs. Gibbons for their sympathy with the work of the schools, and for their kindness in throwing open their grounds for the enjoyment of the children. Mr. Gibbons, in responding, said it had been a great pleasure for him and Mrs. Gibbons to meet the teachers and children of Red Cross-street Schools, in whose welfare they had for a long time taken a deep interest. Three ringing cheers were given for Mr. and Mrs. Gibbons, and a start was made for Wolverhampton. Red Cross-street was reached in safety about nine o'clock, and after singing "Praise God from Whom all Blessings Flow," and giving cheers for their superintendent and teachers, the children dispersed. On Saturday the infants, numbering about 150, had their annual treat. They entered heartily into their juvenile games, and thoroughly enjoyed the good things provided for them.

From the 'Express & Star', Tuesday August 16th 1892

Cakes

[An ommack o'kaerk for tay]

It was customary to have four meals each day, however meagre. Breakfast ranged from a substantial meal of bacon and eggs to just a 'piece of dip' (a slice of bread dipped in bacon liquor). Mid-day dinner was the main meal of the day and again, depending on the family's circumstances was either a hearty meal of plainly cooked meat and vegetables or just a basin of broth. Some children often had just bread and dripping [bread an scrairp it], the dripping being spread on and the majority scraped off again. Tea was almost always bread and jam followed by a slice of cake, and supper was sometimes a light savoury dish or just bread and cheese and a glass of beer. With so many children to cater for at tea time, it was more economical for mothers of large families to bake large plain or fruit cake but occasionally jam tarts, scones, buns and small cakes were made for a special treat. These were almost always eaten piping hot straight from the oven and scoffed as quickly as they could be made.

COCONUT BUNS

6 oz plain flour seived with a little baking powder
2 oz dessicated coconut
2 oz butter
2 oz caster sugar
1 beaten egg
A little milk
6 glacé cherries

Cream the butter and sugar and add the coconut. Add a little of the flour alternatively with the egg and milk and mix well. Put tablespoons of this mixture on to a greased tray. Sprinkle the tops with a little extra coconut, place half a glacé cherry on top and bake about fifteen minutes in a hot oven.

MINT PASTRIES

2 tablespoons currants
1 tablespoon sugar
2 tablespoons finely chopped fresh mint
Shortcrust pastry

Line patty tins with pastry. Mix together all the ingredients and put a teaspoonful of the mixture on to the pastry. Cover with pastry lids and bake in a hot oven for about ten minutes.

RASPBERRY BUNS

½ lb S.R. Flour
2 oz butter
2 oz lard
2 eggs
4 tablespoons sugar
A little jam

Rub the butter and lard into the flour and sugar and add the eggs. Roll the paste about half an inch thick, cut into rounds, place a very small quantity of jam in the middle, turn the edges into the middle and place them upside down on a greased baking tray. Brush the tops with white of an egg and sprinkle with a little caster sugar. Bake for about ten minutes in a hot oven.

COCONUT CAKES

1 Coconut (or 6 oz dessicated coconut)
6 oz caster sugar
2 oz cornflour
2 egg whites

If using a fresh coconut, grate it and dry it slowly in a cool oven. Beat the egg whites stiffly and add the sugar, six ounces of grated coconut and the cornflour. Beat all well together. Drop teaspoons of this mixture on to a sheet of ricepaper or a greased tin and bake in a cool oven until crisp.

LARDY CAKES

1 lb white bread dough
6 oz lard
6 oz mixed dried fruit
6 oz sugar

After the dough has risen, roll into an oblong about twelve inches by eight inches. Cover two thirds with half of the fruit, sugar and lard. Fold the uncovered part over the middle section and then again over the next section. Turn the dough once and repeat the process with the remaining ingredients. After folding for the last time, roll out to fit a baking tin about twelve inches by eight inches. Mark into six squares and bake at Gas mark 6, 400°F for forty-five minutes. When cooked, let the cake stand in the tin for ten minutes to re-absorb the fat. (Not advisable for slimmers)!

Reproduced from the Dudley Almanack

SAUCER TEA CAKES

¼ lb flour
¼ lb fine oatmeal
¼ lb sugar
¼ lb butter
1 egg
2 oz sultanas or raisins
Grated rind of an orange

Rub the butter into the flour, oatmeal and sugar and add the beaten egg, dried fruit and orange rind. Mix well and form into rounds. Place on a greased baking tray, pat flat and bake in a hot oven for about ten minutes.

SCRATCHING CAKE

The ingredients and methods of this recipe are rather vague as each family baked them to suit their own palate and they were, of course, the type of scratchings mentioned on page 61 not hard rind. Mix together equal quantities of breadcrumbs and finely chopped scratchings. To this add sugar, dried fruit, candied peel etcetera, to taste, plus a good pinch of nutmeg. Mix to a soft consistency with beaten egg and/or milk and put into a greased tin. Sprinkle the top with mixed cinnamon and sugar and bake in a moderate oven for about one hour.

BLACK COUNTRY SHORTCAKE

4 oz butter
2 oz caster sugar
2 oz almonds (blanched and chopped)
1 oz angelica (chopped finely)
1 oz glacé cherries (chopped finely)
6 oz flour

Rub the butter and sugar lightly into the flour with the fingertips, add the remaining ingredients and continue mixing until a dough is formed. Shape into a round about half an inch in thickness and place on a greased baking sheet. Prick all over with a fork and mark across into segments. Bake in a moderate oven for about twenty minutes until light golden brown. Allow to cool a little before removing on to a cooling rack. Dust with a little castor sugar and leave until cold.

LITTLE LEMON CHEESECAKES

½ lb Short Crust pastry
¼ lb warmed butter
Peel of 2 lemons
Juice of 1 lemon
¼ lb caster sugar
A few almonds

Cream the butter and sugar until light and fluffy. Add the lemon rind and juice and mix well together. Pour into patty tins lined with the pastry and place a few blanched almonds on the top of each. Bake in a hot oven for about ten minutes.

JOSEPHINE CAKES

½ lb butter
½ lb brown sugar
5 eggs
1 lb flour
½ lb currants
1 glass white wine

Beat the butter and sugar together until light and fluffy. Add the well-beaten eggs and the flour and mix well. Add the currants and sufficient wine to make a soft consistency. Pile into greased patty tins and bake in a moderate oven for approximately ten minutes.

GINGER NOBS

8 oz flour
3 oz margarine
2oz dried fruit
2 tablespoons golden syrup
½ teaspoon Baking Powder
a little ginger
1 egg
2 tablespoons water

Sieve the flour and the baking powder and rub in the margarine. Add the chopped fruit, ginger and the egg. Blend the syrup with the water and mix to a stiff dough. Put on to a greased baking tin in rough heaps. Bake in a hot oven for about twenty minutes.

POTATO SPONGE CAKE

3 oz sugar
2 oz margarine
4 oz flour
1 teaspoon baking powder
1 egg
2 oz mashed potato
2 tablespoons warm milk

Cream the margarine and sugar, and beat in the egg. Fold in the sieved flour and baking powder and lastly, stir in the mashed potato and milk. Put the mixture into two greased sandwich tins and bake in a moderate oven for about twenty minutes. Sandwich together with any filling to hand.

FRUIT BISCUITS

8 oz flour
1 teaspoon Baking powder
A pinch of salt
2 oz margarine
2 oz sultanas or raisins
Milk to mix
2 oz sugar

Mix the salt and sugar into the flour, rub in the margarine. Mix to a very stiff paste with milk. Cut in half and roll out into two squares. Sprinkle the chopped fruit on one half and cover with the other. Roll out again to 1/8 inch thickness. Cut into fingers and bake on a greased baking tray in a moderate oven for about fifteen minutes.

APPLE CHEESE CAKES

4 cooking apples
1 oz golden syrup
1 oz margarine
1 egg
Shortcrust pastry
Grated lemon rind

Peel, core and slice the apples. Stew with the syrup and 1 dessertspoonful of water until tender. Add the margarine and lemon rind. Allow to cool and beat in the egg. Line patty tins with the pastry and put in a little of the mixture. Bake in a moderately hot oven for about 20 minutes.

CHOCOLATE POTATO BUNS

3 oz sugar
2 oz margarine
4 oz flour
2 oz mashed potato
2 eggs
1 oz cocoa
1 level teaspoon baking powder

Cream the margarine and sugar. Mix in the flour sieved with the cocoa and baking powder, then the potatoes and eggs. Put into greased tins and bake in a moderate oven for about fifteen minutes.

POTATO FINGERS

6 oz oatmeal or rolled oats
6 oz mashed potato
2 oz lard
3 oz golden syrup
½ teaspoonful mixed spice
½ teaspoonful cinnamon
1 teaspoonful ground ginger
1 teaspoonful sugar
1 level teaspoonful baking powder

Mix all the dry ingredients, rub in the lard. Add the warmed syrup to make a stiff dough, spread about ¼ inch thick in a greased tin, smooth with a knife. Bake in a moderate oven for about 25 minutes. Leave in the tin to cool then cut into slices.

BEAN TARTS

Shortcrust pastry
4 oz cooked haricot beans
2 oz sugar
2 oz margarine
2 eggs
Almond essence to flavour
A little jam

Cream the sugar and margarine, add the sieved cooked beans, eggs and essence and mix well. Line patty tins with pastry, put a little jam into each one and cover with a layer of the bean mixture. Bake in a moderate oven for about twenty minutes.

CHOCOLATE SPREAD

¼ pint milk
2 oz sugar
1 oz flour
3 oz cocoa

Blend the flour, cocoa and sugar with a little milk, pour over the rest when boiling, return to the pan and stir until smooth and thick, use when cold. This makes a delicious spread on bread and butter or as a filling for a sponge cake.

Glass Engraving Works, Stuart Crystal,
Wordsley, Nr. Stourbridge—B.C.M.

Bare Fist Fight — B.C.M.

Mens' Hobbies and Pastimes

[Werkin ard an playin ard]

Advice given to young Black Country men by their elders:

"Never be ooman licked.
Never back slow osses,
and never let ya navel get tew cloose t'ya backboon"

Working-class women had little time or opportunity to pursue hobbies or pastimes, many being denied activity beyond their own four walls. Any creativity they may have had was suppressed in the endless struggle to rear their children and to make ends meet. Working-class men in the Black Country, however, were renowned for 'working hard and playing hard' and before 1835 when an Act was passed forbidding the baiting of large animals, bear and bull-baiting were an indispensable part of wakes and drew large crowds. Dog-fighting, pigeon-fancying, cock-fighting and bare fist fights were still popular pastimes at the turn of the century, along with foot-running, long-jumping, badger-drawing and rat, beaver, and ferret-fights.

In the Middle Ages, the venue for bull-baiting was often the local churchyard but eventually the Puritans succeeded in limiting the sport to market places where the bull was tethered to a stake fixed in the ground by its owner who charged the owners of the dogs for the privilege of allowing them to run at the bull. The main characteristic of a bull dog is to retain its grip and an attacking dog would grip and hold on until the flesh of the bull came away in its teeth or until its owner prized open the dog's mouth with a stick to release it. Three or four dogs at once were often turned upon a bull but if unlucky enough to get entangled in the bull's horns a dog was tossed high in the air and unless it was caught in the long aprons of the trainers or in blankets held in readiness death often resulted. At the end of the bouts, with the majority of animals ripped to shreds, the bull was slaughtered and the carcass of meat distributed amongst the workers in the crowd.

Pub — Rowley — The 'Ward Arms', Rowley Village. One of the many pubs in the Black Country renowned for its very palatable beer

114

Cock and hens — Fighting cock and
hens belonged to the Author's Father

Cock-Fighting

Without doubt the most popular bloodsport was cockfighting until the
Prevention of Cruelty to Animals Act of 1849 put an end to the sport as
far as public exhibitions were concerned. However, it was still
practised illicitly in screened pits in backyard arenas all over the
Black Country long after it had been outlawed through the passing of
the Act. Prior to this Act, the acknowledged venue in the Black Country
for this 'Sport of Kings and Commoners' was Wednesbury, where a
cross-section of the public including doctors, clergymen and nobility,
gathered to wager as much as four guineas a 'battle' plus forty guineas
for the main match, to watch a brace of spurred cocks tear each other
to pieces in a welter of blood, and to applaud the bravery of the birds.

Cock-fighting has been practised the world over for centuries, the
cock being famed for his courage. It was mentioned in the 'Codes of
Manu' written in India a thousand years before Christ and classic
poets and historians are unanimous in speaking of his valour. Romans

were devoted to the sport and coins and medals are in existance bearing the representation of two fighting cocks stamped upon them. The varieties of Old English Game are legion and include such names as 'Black Reds', 'Spangles', 'Duckwings', 'Blue Reds', 'Duns', 'Muffs' and many more.

When cocks were trimmed for the pit, the hackle, tail and other parts were cut or trimmed but the breast was left intact, hence the birds were described as 'black breasted', or 'smock breasted' as the case may be. Special training was practised from birth, with emphasis on correct diet and on reaching one year of age, the cock's combs and wattles were removed. This was known as being 'dubbed'. A cock was considered mature at two or three years of age when its weight would be between two and a half and three and a half pounds. The following saying held sway in most Black country sporting arenas at the time:

[An ounce tew a fowl is a pound tew a dog an a stoon tew a mon]

Prior to the fight the bird's feathers were clipped. More intensive training was given about a week or ten days before the fight, and immediately before being put into the pit, metal spurs were fitted over the natural spurs.

Over the years, spurs have been made from iron, brass, steel or silver, the latter having a portion of copper in their composition, making them stronger and more flexible. All matches of importance were fought in silver as they were not so immediately destructive as steel. This enabled the birds to show their powers of endurance more fully.

The act of 'heeling' a game cock consisted of fixing the silver spurs over the natural spurs which had previously been cut off to about one inch of the leg, the point extending back on a line with the outside of the hock, outside the line of the natural spur. If fixed too far towards the outside, the blows would be ineffectual, while if set too far in, it would cause the cock to cut his own throat. The spurs were padded firm at the socket and secured firmly with cobbler's waxed thread. If they came off in a fight they were not allowed to be replaced. At the same time, if too tight, they would cramp the cock. With the spurs secured, the birds were then placed in the pit to fight to the death.

The following rhyme was a popular drinking toast in the Black Country at the turn of the century and was often quoted by my father.

"Here's to the tot and the bottle,
Here's to a drink on the sly,
I mean to wet my old throttle,
and live like a cock till I die".

IN THE BOROUGH OF KIDDERMINSTER, IN THE COUNTY OF WORCESTER.

To [illegible] of the Borough of Kidderminster aforesaid. [illegible]

Information has been laid this day by Edwin Bennett and each of you for that you on the 29th day of September 1906, at the Borough of Kidderminster aforesaid, unlawfully did use a certain Room situate at York Street in the said Borough of Kidderminster for the purpose of fighting cocks

contrary to the Statute in such case made and provided.

You and each of you **are therefore** hereby summoned to appear before the Court of Summary Jurisdiction, sitting at the Police Court, Town Hall, in the said Borough of Kidderminster, on **Friday**, the 5th day of October 1906 at the hour of Eleven o'clock in the forenoon, to answer to the said information.

Dated the 1st day of October One Thousand Nine Hundred and six

Part I.—No. 2.
Summary Jurisdiction
Summons to Defendant

Thomas Grove
Justice of the Peace for the Borough aforesaid.

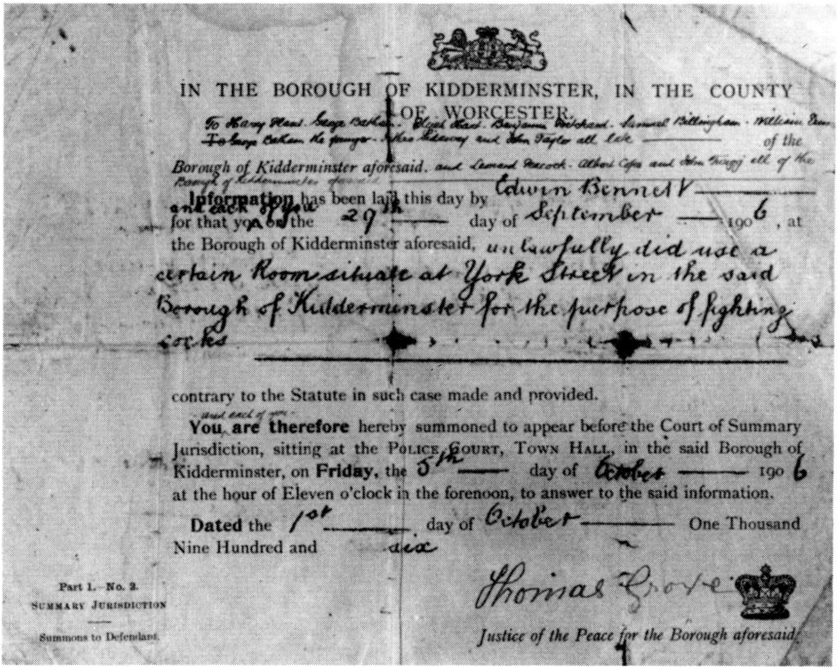

Summons — Belonged to Author's father

Novel Football Match on Dudley Town Football Field, for the benefit of the Guest Hospital, between the Members of Mrs Levey's Pantomime Company and eleven local tradesmen wearing silk hats. The proceeds were £20.

Reproduced from the Dudley Almanack

Articles of Agreement made on ___12___ day of _April_ in 9_1_

David Brindly, Black dog _M, Ger Sual Dog_ agrees to fight his _____ pounds weight against

___Powell dog 30 lbs___ Dog _Brindly_ Dog _30 lbs_

_____ pounds weight, for £ _10_ aside at _____

on the _____ day of _____ 18___ The dogs to be

weighed at _____ o'clock in the _____ and fight between _____

o'clock in the _____

The deposits to be made as hereinafter noted: to be delivered to _Charles Newma_

(who is the final Stakeholder), namely, the first deposit of £ _5_ aside at the making of the

Match; the second Deposit of £ _2 10_ _gdr_ on the _____ of _May_

at the house of _____ : Third Deposit of £ _____ on the _____

of _____ at the house of _____

_____ on the _____ of _____ at the house of _____

and the Fifth Deposit of £ _____ on the _____ of _____ at the house

of _a deposit 2.10_ which is the last. _on the day of fight_

RULES. _on monen 17 of may_

1st.—To be a fair fight   yards from the scratch

2nd.—Both Dogs to be tasted before and after fighting if required.

3rd.—Both Dogs to be shewn fair to the scratch, and washed at their own corners.

4th.—Both seconds to deliver the Dogs fair at the corner, and not leave until the Dogs commence fighting.

5th.—A Referee to be chosen in the pit; one minute time to be allowed between every fair go away; fifty seconds allowed for sponging; and at the expiration of that time the time-keeper shall call make ready, and as soon as the minute is expired the Dogs to be delivered and the Dog refusing or stopping on the way to be the Loser.

6th.—Should either second pick his dog up in a mistake, he shall put it down immediately, by order of the Referee, or the money to be forfeited.

7th.—Should anything pernicious be found on either Dog, before or after fighting in the pit, the backers of the Dog so found to forfeit, and the person holding the battle money to give it up immediately, when called upon to do so.

8th.—Referee to be chosen in the pit before fighting, whose decision in all cases shall be final.

10th.—In any case of a Dog being declared dead, the Referee, the living Dog shall remain and be ____ minutes, when he shall be taken to his corner if it be its turn to scratch, or if it be the dead Dogs turn the Fight shall be at an end by order of the Referee.

11th.—In case of Police interference the Referee to name the next place and time of fighting, on the same day if possible, and day by day until it be decided, but if no referee be chosen, the Stakeholder to name the next place and time; but if a referee has been chosen and then refuses to name the next place and time of fighting, or goes away after being disturbed, then the power of chusing the place of fighting shall be left with the Stakeholder, and a fresh Referee to be chosen in the pit, and the power of the former one to be entirely gone.

12th.—In case of Police interference and the Dogs have commenced fighting they will not be required to weigh any more; but if they have not commenced fighting they will have to weigh day by day at ____ lbs. until decided at the time and place named by the Referee, or if he refuses or goes away then the Stakeholder has to name the time and place.

13th.—The seconder of either Dog is upon no consideration to call his adversary's Dog by name while in the pit, nor use anything whatever in his hands with which to call off his Dog.

14th.—To toss up the night before fighting for the place of fighting, between the hours of ____ and ____ o'clock, at the house where the last deposit is made.

15th.—The above stakes are not to be given up until fairly won or lost by a fight, unless either party break the above agreement.

16th.—All deposits to be made between the hour of ____ and ____ o'clock at night.

17th.—Either party not following up or breaking the above agreements, to forfeit the money down.

David Brindly +
George Powel +

Witnesses | **Signed** |

Dog Rules — B.C.M.

Dog Fighting

The Staffordshire Bull Terrier was and still is the breed of dog most associated with the Black Country. After 1835 when the baiting of large animals was outlawed, dog-fighting became more popular. Because bull dogs were not agile enough in a sport where swiftness of movement was often the deciding factor, breeders of the day crossed the smaller bull dogs with the now extinct Old English Terrier which resulted in a dog known as the Bull Dog Terrier, Bull and Terrier or Pitbull Terrier.

The present day Staffordshire Bull Terrier evolved from such dogs with careful and selective breeding by enthusiasts in the Black Country. Through their efforts the breed eventually became established and registered by the Kennel Club. Working-class owners of a fighting dog supplemented their meagre earnings by wagers placed on the dog which often resulted in dogs being entered to fight when they had not fully recovered from a previous bout.

Pigeon Fancying

By comparison, pigeon fancying was a much gentler sport and is still a favourite pastime for scores of Black Country men, despite the rigid planning laws governing the erection of lofts. Men with relatively small garden space could keep pigeons, and racing them at weekends was the highlight of the week. Rigorous training was necessary from when the pigeons were youngsters until they were mature enough to be entered for racing; special attention being paid to diet, as success in long-distance racing depended upon the physique of the bird. At about a week old, a metal ring with a serial number for identification was placed on the pigeon's leg. At different stages in their development a racing team of birds were placed in a basket by their owners, taken to an open space a few miles from home and then released 'tossed' to

make their way back to their lofts. The distance was increased during the training period until they were ready to be entered for racing longer distances.

Each pigeon-fancier belonged to a club, invariably the local pub, where the birds were taken at racing events and handed over to the officials, along with a race sheet containing details of the bird and pools money, a form of betting. The identification number on the metal ring was registered and an expandable rubber ring, also numbered, was secured to the bird's leg. All the assembled birds were placed together in baskets which were then taken to the nearest railway station for transportation. Today, this is done by road transport. Throughout the journey the birds were fed and watered at regular intervals. Each fancier had his own racing clock and prior to the race all the clocks were synchronized with a master clock in the local clubhouse, and then sealed. This was vital, as a race could be won or lost by a split second.

On the day of the race the assembled birds were released to start their often gruelling flight back to their own lofts which were distinguishable from a distance by being painted in a striped effect with two contrasting colours, usually black and white. Many birds were lost on these journeys especially those transported to the Continent, when sea mist and fog on the English Channel made their homeward flight hazardous. Sitting quietly and patiently outside his loft, the fancier anxiously awaited the arrival of his birds. In adverse weather conditions the pigeons flew low and entered the loft almost unnoticed but on a clear day they could be detected when they were only a speck in the sky. The most rewarding moment of the sport was when a pigeon, recognising his loft, folded its wings before plummetting through the air and landing. The rubber ring attached to the leg of the bird was then deftly removed and fitted into a metal furrule which in turn was placed in the clock and struck by means of a lever on the side, recording the exact time of arrival. The speed at which this was done was incredible as so much depended on split-second timing.

The clocks were taken to the clubhouse and unsealed one at a time in the presence of the officials who recorded each timing before announcing the winner. The clubhouse rules specified a set time for the clocks to be returned as it was not unknown for them to be tampered with and the timing adjusted to the owner's advantage, so immediately the pigeon had been clocked in, the owner had to run as fast as possible to return the clock, frequently in the rougher quarters to be waylaid by groups of men with bets on other pigeons.

As with most sports and pastimes, money was a necessary evil when racing pigeons but many fanciers with no money to spare would still keep a kit of 'tumblers' to enjoy in their leisure hours. These pigeons were exercised outside, around the loft and on fine days reached tremendous heights until they were just a speck in the sky. A 'tumbler' is a breed of pigeon which stops in mid-flight and performs an acrobatic tumbling roll.

Before long-distance pigeon racing became popular, Sunday, for the less devout was a day for 'milers'. This was a pastime in which twenty or so men from the same area competed in a form of short-distance, low-flying pigeon racing. An agreed distance approximately 500 yards to a mile was paced out from the lofts of each competitor to the place where the birds were to be released and any obstacles such as long grass and small banks [knobs] were removed along the route prior to the race, to enable the birds to be unhindered in their flight. Ever anxious to return to their mate in their nesting box, the birds, when released, just skimmed the roofs of the houses and in some cases would take a short cut through the entry dividing houses of this type.

Times were established by stop-watch, with one official setting the time the birds were released and another official noting the time of arrival, with the remaining competitiors as onlookers. Although the actual race of each bird took only minutes, it took all day to get around all the lofts recording the exact time of each bird and establishing the winner. Surprisingly, sovereigns were often to be seen amongst the bettings and punches were frequently thrown if there was a discrepancy in the final decision. The more unscrupulous owners thought nothing of encouraging groups of sightseers along the route to ["throw ya coots up to frighten em"].

This pastime of pigeon-flying in which many Black Country men indulged meant that stocks eventually had to be reduced and the surplus pigeons were of course utilized for family meals.

Carnival Race — By kind permission of Walter Taylor

Photo shows the proprietor of the George and Dragon public house, High Street, Blackheath, Rowley Regis, together with Bill Taylor, John Taylor, and George Hill (Secretary of the Blackheath and District Homing Society), on the occasion of an Annual Pigeon Race in the early nineteen hundreds, when a pig's carcase was one of the prizes along with the gold medals

PIGEON PIE

3 or 4 pigeons
1 lb shin of beef
1 large onion
Salt and pepper
Flaky or puff pastry
Beef dripping or cooking oil for frying

(Sufficient for four)

The only meaty part of a pigeon is the breast — the legs usually being discarded. Fry the onion until soft and transfer to a pie dish with a pie funnel placed in the middle. Cut the pigeon breasts and shin into small pieces and brown in the remaining dripping. Add to the onions, season with salt and pepper and cover with a pastry lid. Brush with egg yolk or milk and bake for about one hour in a medium oven.

JUGGED PIGEON (Method 1)

4 pigeons
2 hard-boiled egg yolks
A sprig of parsley
The grated rind of half a lemon
4 oz suet
The weight of the livers in suet and breadcrumbs
Salt and pepper
A trace of nutmeg
1 egg
2 oz softened butter
1 head of celery
A glass of white wine
A bunch of sweet herbs
4 cloves
2 blades of mace

(Sufficient for four)

Draw and clean the pigeons. Boil the livers for a few minutes and then mince them finely with the egg yolks, grated lemon rind, suet, breadcrumbs, parsley, salt, pepper and nutmeg. Mix well together with the beaten egg and the butter. Stuff the pigeons with this forcemeat, sew up the vents and dip the pigeons into warm water. Sprinkle over them some salt and pepper and place in a stew jar together with the celery, herbs, cloves, mace, and wine. Cover the jar closely and stand in a pan of boiling water for three hours, taking care the water does not get to the top of the jar. After three hours, strain the gravy into a small saucepan, stir in a little butter rolled in flour, boil it up until it is thick and pour it over the pigeons. Garnish with lemon.

JUGGED PIGEON   (Method 2)

4 pigeon breasts
1 lb shin of beef
1 large onion
1 parsnip
2 carrots
1 small swede or turnip
½ pt cooking wine

(Elderberry wine was used in the Black Country as these trees grew in abundance and full use was made of them).

1 pint of stock
1 bay leaf

(Sufficient for two)

Dice the vegetables and place in a stew jar or casserole dish. Lay the pigeon breasts on top of the vegetables, season and cover with wine and stock. Add the bay leaf and cook gently in a moderate oven for about three hours.

STEWED PIGEON

3 large pigeons (halved)
1 small onion stuck with cloves
Bouquet garni made from:
Strips of lemon peel

6 peppercorns
and a small bunch of parsley
Stock to cover
Flour or cornflour to thicken

(Sufficient for four)

Place all the ingredients in a stewjar and stew very slowly for about two hours. Thicken towards the end of cooking time with flour or cornflour and water, and serve with peas and potatoes.

Rabbit

Rabbit was a very popular form of protein in the Black Country, as elsewhere, at the turn of the century. There was an abundance of wild rabbits in the surrounding countryside and most boys and men from working-class backgrounds were adept in the art of rabbit-snaring, often out of necessity. Many men used just an oversize catapult. A good rich stew could be made from a rabbit, half a pound of stewing steak and a variety of vegetables such as swedes, carrots, turnips and leeks all combined in a stewjar and left to simmer in a slow oven for a couple of hours, or alternatively in a large pot over the fire. This stew would sometimes be thickened towards the end of cooking time but either way was easy to prepare and could be left to cook with little attention. The following recipes, however, are a little more varied.

RABBIT BRAWN

1 Rabbit (cut into joints)
2 pig's trotters
1 bay leaf
Salt and pepper
2 hard-boiled eggs

(Sufficient for four)

Cover the rabbit, trotters, bay leaf and seasoning with water, bring to the boil and simmer for about two hours. Leave in the juices until cool. Remove the meat from the bones, chop up finely and place the mixture on to rings of hard-boiled egg previously placed in a mould or basin. Spoon a little of the juices over and cover with a saucer, placing a weight on top to compress the mixture. Chill in the refrigerator before turning out of the dish and serve with salad or pickles.

RABBIT PUDDING

1 Rabbit (cut into joints)
½ lb diced lean pork
Seasoned flour
Suet crust

(Sufficient for four)

Coat the rabbit joints and pork in the seasoned flour and place in a suet crust-lined basin. Cover with water and then a lid of suet crust. Cover with greased paper and a cloth and steam for at least two hours. Serve with vegetables of your choice.

ROAST RABBIT

1 Rabbit
Forcemeat made from:
minced liver and heart of the rabbit, combined with two ounces
of shredded suet, approximately one pound of fresh breadcrumbs,
two beaten eggs, thyme, parsley, lemon juice, salt and pepper

(Sufficient for four)

Thoroughly wash the rabbit, wipe dry and line inside with forcemeat. Sew the rabbit up and skewer the legs and shoulders close to the body. Wrap the rabbit in buttered paper or tin foil and bake in a medium oven for about one hour. Before serving, flour the rabbit and baste with a spoonful of melted butter and return it to the oven until nicely browned. Serve with vegetables of your choice, gravy and red-currant jelly.

RABBIT PIE

1 Rabbit (cut into joints)
¼ lb Streaky bacon
1 onion (sliced and fried)
1 Breakfastcup of stock
Salt and pepper
½ teaspoon powdered mace
Puff pastry

(Sufficient for four)

Place all the ingredients except the pastry in a basin, cover with a plate and bake in the oven for about one hour. Remove to cool, cover with the pastry and bake for another half an hour. Sprinkle a little chopped parsley over the finished dish before serving.

STEWED RABBIT AND SAUSAGE

1 Rabbit (cut into joints)
½ lb sausages (cut into one inch lengths)
1 Spanish onion (sliced)
1 Carrot (diced)
Salt and pepper

(Sufficient for four)

Place all the ingredients into a saucepan, cover with water, bring to the boil and simmer gently for about two hours. When cooked, thicken with a little flour or cornflour, gravy browning and water.

FEB. 7 1893
Frightful Accident to Coal Pickers at Cradley Heath—two women buried in a disused pit mound.

Reproduced from the Dudley Almanack

JUGGED RABBIT

1 Rabbit (cut into joints)
1 Onion
Elderberry wine
Redcurrant Jelly
Salt and pepper
Flour or cornflour to thicken
Mixed herbs

(Sufficient for four)

Fry the onion until soft and then the rabbit until lightly browned. Place in a stewjar and cover with wine. Add a little red currant jelly, salt and pepper and herbs. Thicken with flour or cornflour and water and stew gently until tender.

RABBIT CUSTARD PIE

1 Rabbit (cut into joints)
2 eggs
3 teacups of milk
½ pint stock
1 teaspoon chopped parsley
1 minced onion
½ lb puff pastry

(Sufficient for four)

Stew or boil the rabbit until tender. Remove the bones and place the meat in a dish. Mix together the eggs, milk, stock, parsley and onion and pour over the rabbit pieces. Cover with pastry and bake in a moderate oven for about one hour. This pie is best eaten cold.

Shocking death of a child named Beatrice Ann Dews, of Upper Gornal, by being run over by a horse and cart

Reproduced from the Dudley Almanack

Childrens' Games and Pastimes

[Keep out o'thos road]

With a warning cry from their mothers to [Keep out o'thos road], children, when not at school or work, gathered in the streets to 'play', only returning home for meals or at dusk which was heralded by the lamplighter. Children of mixed ages gathered in groups, with older girls acting as 'mother' to the babies and younger brothers and sisters, giving their mothers a little respite from their daily drudgery. Nearly everyone had a nickname, many related to personal peculiarities, and this applied to adults as well as children. Names like 'Shady Hackett', 'Cabbage', 'Duffy', 'Nerk', 'Flannel Jesus', 'Sammy Pigiron', 'Billy on th'ob', 'Harry Cabbage', 'Albert Ardmate' (butcher), 'Ode tile', 'Dragon', 'Tummy and Billy Rot', and 'Joey Sixfoot' (undertaker), the majority of them being larger than life characters.

To be left-handed was to be known as [caggy onded] and slow-witted people were called [noggan yeds]. Even fields and meadows were known by such names as 'Little Hocks field', 'Big Hocks field', 'The Martins', etcetera. Only men carried pocket 'fob' watches but children knew the time of day by the sound of the factory 'bulls' or 'sirens' which punctually gave a few minutes warning to workers on their way to work. They were also a sign for the workers to stop for a dinner break and to mark the end of different shifts. Children were seldom bored and because the streets were free from the dangers and hazards of today's traffic, were never at a loss for street games, a selection of which follow, and these unsophisticated games were played for hours without having to repeat one.

Here we go round the Mulberry bush.
Tip Cat
Wallflowers, wallflowers growing up so high.
Hop Scotch
Here we come gathering nuts in May
Five Jacks
Spinning tops and whips.
Jack upon the mopstick.
Kick the can.
Ring a ring-o-roses.
Tug-o-war.
Poor Mary sits a weeping
Blind man's buff.
Tick.
Hide and Seek.
Chalk Chase.
Release.
The farmer wants a wife.
Oranges and lemons.
In and out the darking bluebells.
Sheep, sheep come over.
Statues.
Aunties and Uncles.
and many others.

Children devised their own amusements. Following horse-drawn vehicles armed with a bucket and shovel to collect horse-droppings [oss

Children with pushchair —by kind permission of Marilyn McDougall

muck] which was sold for a few coppers to "force the rhubarb" [roobub], was one way of earning a little extra pocket money. Children also earned money topping and tailing swedes and mangles for use as cattle food, on the few remaining isolated farms, but what little spare time they had was kept mainly for pleasure. Peashooters and whistles were made from ground elder stems (goutweed), after the pith had been removed and a common sound reverberating through the streets was children singing and whistling to the accompaniment of bones, salvaged from joints of boiled ribs of beef. These flat bones which were about six inches long by one and a half inches wide were placed between the fingers and rattled together to resemble a tune. They were called 'clappers' and no self-respecting boy would be without a set in his pocket. An expression [gooin like the clappers] meaning 'a swift movement', had its origin here.

Two blades of thick grass placed between the thumbs and blown into produced a shrill whistling sound. Alternatively, a comb wrapped in thin paper could be blown upon to make a similar sound. Children with a real flair for music, mastered the art of playing the 'spoons' when two dessert-spoons were balanced between their fingers and rattled together as they were rolled up and down the player's arms and thighs. These then were the makeshift musical instruments of the children of less affluent families. Most boys carried penknives and catapults which were rarely used for aggression but from time to time raids between rival gangs erupted and then the use of catapults and stone-throwing became the tactics.

Each season occasioned different games. In the Spring there was bird-nesting, while the Autumn saw children scrummaging amongst the hedges for blackberries which were collected in jam jars with string handles. At least half the pickings were eaten before they had time to reach the jar and unless the remainder were taken home to be made into a blackberry pie or bramble jelly, the children pounded them with a piece of hawthorn stripped of the bark, and known as a 'jabber', to make a syrup drink.

During the summer months, children formed little gangs and went in search of pignuts, 'poor mans truffles', an edible tuber buried in the ground in meadows. These, when rubbed clean were considered a great delicacy, and although practically extinct now in the Black Country could once be found in abundance. Children also ate raw carrots, swedes, turnips and even potatoes. These vegetables were just rubbed on a brick wall to remove the outer skin and dirt and eaten 'as sweet as a nut'. Raw vegetables were, of course, better for the children than unlimited supplies of sweets and chocolate, and surprisingly, few children came to any harm with the apparent lack of hygiene. Visits to a dentist were virtually non-existant.

When children did have enough pocket money for sweets [suck], the favourites of the day were troachdrops, bulls-eyes, brandy-balls, butter-drops, dolly-mixtures, acid-drops and pear-drops, gob-stoppers, sherbet-dabs and rock, but as an alternative, a stick of rhubarb dipped in a small twist of sugar in newspaper was eaten with great relish. It was also not uncommon for children to chew liquorice wood, tallow candles and even tar salvaged from road works.

Photo supplied by Jim Aldridge

A fair proportion of the sweet shops were 'front room shops' with homemade fittings and where supplies of sweets were stored in chests of drawers. The different varieties were so arranged that the cheaper sweets were kept in the bottom drawer and the more expensive in the top ones. Children were then able to ask for [an a'penny look'o tha drawa], and were allowed to rummage amongst the different varieties before making their final decision. Looking in the drawer was part of the fun.

Groups of girls meandered through the fields in summer in search of different varieties of wild flowers which grew in profusion then, but many of which have now diminished in number. These included primroses, cross-irons, ladies-sore-fingers, green-sal, buttercups, bluebells, harebells, cowslips, cow-parsley, cuckoo-flowers, clover, tufted-vetch, meadowsweet, rosebay-willow-herb, forget-me-not, bindweed, foxgloves, eyebright, ragwort, colt's-foot, celandines. dandelions, yellow kingcups (water blubbers), daisies and of course poppies.

A garland of daisy-chains, patiently made to adorn a girl, instantly transformed her into an imaginery princess and held more meaning for her than the finest jewels. 'Milk' was sucked from clover petals and 'honey' from honeysuckle, and a buttercup held under one's chin, casting a yellow shadow to the throat, supposedly denoted to what degree one liked butter. The young leaves of the hawthorn bush were eaten as 'bread and cheese' and girls made collections of flowerheads, grasses and ferns, pressed between book pages to study and ponder over during the long winter nights.

Boys romped the fields hunting butterflies which were then kept on a cabbage leaf in a jam jar, sometimes to be freed later in the day but more often than not were secured to a board with a knob pin along with other varieties, plus moths [bob owlers] and dragon flies [oss 'ornets]. With very few toys, these collections of butterflies and pressed flowers became treasured personal possessions. Boys spent hours flying kites which were always homemade from tissue or newspaper and thin strips of wood.

Children steered hoops [boughles] in the streets and ropes were secured around the ladder arms of street lamp-posts to make swings for the girls. Long ropes stretching the full width of the road from one blue pavior brick pavement edged with cast-iron or Rowley Rag stone-

Bushbury Lane, Wolverhampton — Wolverhampton Reference Library

kerbing, to the opposite pavement, were used for skipping games with girls chanting songs like 'Eva Weaver,' 'The big ship sails', 'All in together girls', 'Sally go round the sun', and 'Salt, pepper mustard, vinegar' when emphasis was placed on 'vinegar' and the rope turned twice for one jump. Similar group-skipping across the full width of the road was an enjoyable way for girls to get to local recreational beauty spots. They were able to skip miles without fear of interruption by traffic. Ball games were played against any vacant brick wall with the children chanting songs like *One, two three, O'Larer* as they performed a sequence of movements under arms and legs and spinning round before catching the ball.

At the onset of winter, the majority of boys and some girls pierced holes in empty tin cans and secured long handles of wire around them. These were then filled with red hot 'gledes' and topped with pieces of coal or coke and were known as fire cans. The top of the cans were left open and as the cans were swung in a figure of eight movement, the fire was kept alight and glowed in the dark.

BOROUGH OF DUDLEY.

Removal of Night Soil Manure,
AND HOUSEHOLD ASHES AND RUBBISH.

IMPORTANT NOTICE.

THE TOWN COUNCIL of this Borough HEREBY GIVE NOTICE that they have entered into three several Contracts for the Removal of Night Soil Manure, and Household Ashes and Rubbish, throughout the Borough, for a period of Twelve Calendar Months, from the 2nd day of March, 1869, the Cost of which will be paid out of the Rates.

ALL PERSONS
REQUIRING THEIR PRIVIES, CESSPOOLS, AND ASHPITS EMPTIED,
Are requested to Give Notice

TO MR. H. SMITHEMAN

The Inspector of Nuisances, in the following form, a separate Notice to be given for each Premises, (namely) :—

BOROUGH OF DUDLEY.

TO THE INSPECTOR OF NUISANCES.

I HEREBY GIVE YOU NOTICE that I require the Night Soil Manure, and Household Ashes and Rubbish, Emptied and Removed from the undermentioned Premises.

Name of Occupier.	Number of the House, and Name of the Street or Place where the Privy, Cesspool and Ashpit, are situated.

Dated . 1869. (Signed) _____ Occupier.

N.B.—When properly filled up the above Notice may be either delivered at the Inspector of Nuisances' Office, Corporation Buildings, 2, Priory Street, Dudley, on any day (except Sunday) between the hours of 9 and 11 in the Morning, or may be sent to him *Post Paid*, through the post. *All Notices must be in writing, and where the above Form is not used, they must contain the information required in such Form, otherwise they will not be received or attended to.*

Printed Forms of Notice may be had by any Occupier, free of charge, at the following Places, on any day (except Sunday), between the hours of 9 and 11 in the Morning, *(namely)* :—

The Inspector of Nuisances' Office, Corporation Buildings, 2, Priory Street, Dudley.
The Police Station, 24, Brown Street, Kates Hill.
The Police Station, 67, Dixon's Green.
The Police Station, 5, Holly Hall.
The Police Stations, Netherton, namely:—25 and 26, Castle Street, 14, Chapel Street, Primrose Hill, and 60, Quarry Bank Road, Dudley Wood.

On receipt of a Notice, as above, the Inspector of Nuisances will give the necessary directions to the Contractor in whose District the Premises are situated, who will Empty and Remove the Night Soil Manure, and Household Ashes and Rubbish,

FREE OF CHARGE.

The Contractors will make a charge for the REMOVAL OF BUILDER'S RUBBLE, and WASTE MATERIALS, ENGINE MUFFLE, and STOVE, or other CINDERS and RUBBISH, not being Night Soil Manure, or Household Ashes and Rubbish.

BY ORDER,

W. H. BROOKE,

TOWN CLERK, & CLERK TO THE LOCAL BOARD OF HEALTH.

Town Clerk's Offices,
206, Wolverhampton St., Dudley, 22nd April, 1869.

JOHN LUKIS, "Guardian" Steam Printing Works, Phœnix Buildings, Hall Street, Dudley.

Today this practice would be considered highly dangerous as the cans were often suspended just a little too long in the air causing the red-hot embers to fall out, often down the neck of the child swinging the fire can but in those days this pastime was eagerly looked forward to in the winter evenings. Boys fished for tiddlers, tadpoles and 'jack bannocks' in the many marl holes and pools and of course, most boys learned to swim in the same pools or the local stretch of the canal. Frozen pools in disused quarries became ice rinks and icy footpaths became a series of glassy slides, highly dangerous to walk on but giving endless pleasure to children in the long winter months.

At night, while children lay sleeping, a gruesome but very necessary task was being carried out by the night soil men [night silers] who collected and disposed of the accumulated excrement of each household. There were few flush lavatories, merely earth or ash closets, one often being shared by several families. A simple wooden seat, usually with two suitably-shaped holes was suspended over the ash pit. At intervals, waste was removed by wheelbarrow through the entries dividing the houses and in some houses without entries through the living quarters and dumped in the roads for collection by horse and cart.

A circle of lime measuring approximately six feet in diameter and several inches high was strewn on the road beforehand to contain the waste and make it drier for the night soil men to shovel on to the carts for disposal. Although this operation took place mainly at night and in the early hours, there were still tell-tale signs in the form of damp patches enclosed in a white circle remaining in the streets when the children made their way to school, making it hard to resist the temptation to jump over these en-route. It was in fact considered a game!

THE NIGHT SOIL DEPOT AT NETHERTON.

Alderman JOHN DUNN drew the attention of the Council to the position of the night soil depot at Netherton, which should be altered without delay.

Councillor ELEY endorsed the remarks of the previous speaker, and urged the Council to take steps at once with a view to an improvement.

Councillor ROUND also appreciated the necessity for an alteration in the existing state of affairs, pointing out that scarlet fever was rife in the neighbourhood.

On the MAYOR promising that the subject should have the careful consideration of the Sanitary Committee of the Council, the matter dropped.

From 'The Midland Sun' Saturday April 15th 1893

Beverages

[When yome as dry as a Lime Burner's Clog]

"Thuz many a good raizon for drinkin
An one'uz just entered me yed,
If yo cor ave a drink when yome livin'
'ow the 'ell can ya drink when yome jed."

Most manual workers in the Black Country were heavy beer drinkers, many brewing their own supply in the wash-house, invariably known in the Black Country as the 'brewhouse' [brewus], a small building situated a few yards from the kitchen door and containing a black grate, boiler and sink. Methods of brewing varied from family to family but the end product was usually very potent and when anyone said they were 'craw-stalled' it meant they were extremely thirsty.

The brewhouse was also used for baking the family's weekly supply of bread and women spent practically all day in the brewhouse on Mondays, doing the family wash. This was an ordeal with no modern equipment, just a wooden or zinc washtub, a 'maid' or 'dolly' for pounding out the dirt in the soiled garments and a huge mangle with wooden rollers for wringing out the excess water. Hot water was obtained by lighting a fire under the wash boiler situated in one corner of the brewhouse, though a calamity often resulted if the wind

Chump Dolly

was blowing in the wrong direction, causing havoc with the fire and as a consequence, taking the water longer to heat.

Despite the simple equipment, and the fact that they had to stop at intervals to get their breath back before re-commencing, women washed, boiled, blued, starched and ironed the garments and managed to produce an end result with which they could be proud. The sound of women 'maiding' on washday (always Monday) sounded like the beating of tom-toms. Pregnant women approaching labour were often recommended to "do some maiding, to help you on". If inclement weather prevented the clothes being dried out of doors, they were slung on a clothes line suspended above the fire grate or dried on the fender in front of the fire. The smell of mounds of washing being dried this way hung in the nostrils for days and once experienced was never forgotten.

Non-alcholic beverages for children were also made in the brewhouse and the following drinks were particularly refreshing. Nettle pop was made from young nettles easily obtained from the roadside or fields round about. This was made in abundance in the early Spring and although capable of remaining fresh for several weeks, rarely lasted that long. In fact, additional supplies were made at regular intervals all through the summer.

NETTLE POP

A generous handful of nettle tops
(hands of course protected
with gloves)

1 lemon
2 or 3 sticks of rhubarb
A small piece of root ginger
1 oz Yeast
¾ lb sugar

In a large saucepan, boil the nettles, rhubarb, ginger and lemon in about one gallon of water and leave to simmer gently for about one hour. Strain the liquid into a bucket or large basin, add the sugar and stir until dissolved. Leave the liquid to cool and when lukewarm, sprinkle the yeast on top and cover with a lid, when fermentation will take place. After about two days, syphon the liquid into screw-top bottles and leave for a further five to six days when it will then be ready for drinking. Care is needed when opening these bottles as it can sometimes be very fizzy. The sediment which accumulates in the bottom of the bottle is usually discarded, so care is needed when pouring.

Elderberries, found in abundance in the Black Country were utilized both in cooking, wine-making and health giving remedies. The rich juicy berries and elderflowers made excellent wine and the flowerheads were a splendid ingredient for the following recipe:

ELDERFLOWER 'CHAMPAGNE'

2/3 heads of elderflower in full bloom
1½ lbs sugar
1 lemon, quartered
1 gallon of cold water

Combine all the ingredients in a large container and leave for twenty-four hours, after which time, strain and bottle in screw-top bottles. This is a delicious sparkling drink, and very refreshing.

The longer these effervescent drinks are kept, the fizzier they become and if kept too long can cause bottles to explode, so small quantities, used within a few weeks is by far the best method. Care should be exercised when opening. A tea cloth covering the bottle will prevent any overflow. Originally, corks tied down with string were used not screw-tops, so that any build up of gasses would force the cork to pop out and prevent the bottles breaking.

LEMON SQUASH

Rind and juice of 2 lemons
2 lbs sugar
1 quart boiling water
1¼ oz citric acid
3 tbsp White wine vinegar

Pour the water over the sugar, lemon rind and juice and stir. When cool, add citric acid and bottle. Dilute to drink.

SUMMER FRUIT DRINK

6 lbs of mixed fruit: raspberries, strawberries, red and
blackcurrants, gooseberries, etc.
2½ oz tartaric acid
1½ lbs sugar
Water

Dissolve the tartaric acid in the water, pour it over the fruit (slightly bruised) and let it stand for twenty-four hours. Strain off the juice and to every pint add one and a half pounds of sugar. Let the sugar dissolve without any heat and then pour carefully into bottles, using a funnel. Cork and store in a cool place. Dilute to drink.

LEMON SYRUP

3 large lemons
1 oz citric acid
2 lbs sugar
3 pints of water

Peel the lemons thinly and boil the peel in the water for an hour. Add the juice and boil for a further quarter of an hour. Strain through muslin, return to the pan, add the citric acid and sugar and boil until the sugar has dissolved (about five minutes). When cool, bottle for use. Dilute to drink.

RASPBERRY CORDIAL

12 breakfast cups of cold water
½ oz tartaric acid
3 lbs raspberries
Sugar

Dissolve the tartaric acid in the water and pour it over the fruit. Let it stand for twenty-four hours, then strain through a jelly bag. Measure the juice and to each breakfastcupful add half a pound of sugar. Mix well and bottle. Dilute to drink.

WINTER DRINK

1½ oz essence of ginger
¾ oz essence of cayenne
2 oz tartaric acid
6 lbs lump sugar
2 gallons of boiling water

Put the water on to the above ingredients, leave to get cold and then add a few drops of burnt sugar to colour it. Bottle and cork tightly. Ready for use in a few days. Excellent as it is or with a little warm water.

Dudley Station (No longer in existence)

File-Making, Vaughan Bross, Hope Works, Dudley—B.C.M.

Life in General

[Meckin the moost on it]

["God's good and tha Daval aye altogetha ta bad"]

Bread was the staple food in the Black Country and was utilized in many ways. Toast or just bread in a basin with tea or milk poured over was eaten as a cereal by lots of children and some men were known to place cubes of toast on top of a pint of beer, which served as a filler between meals. A substitute for coffee in some areas was bread, burnt black and then ground.

To replace the liquid lost through the sweat of arduous toil, often in the vicinity of raging furnaces, manual workers would stop for a break or a 'tune' several times during the day, a bottle of cold tea being the next most popular beverage to beer. Workmen and women took a supply of tea, sugar and condensed milk (Jolly Boy was a popular brand). Tea and sugar were sprinkled on a piece of newspaper and a tablespoon of condensed milk was dropped into the centre of this with

143

NO GO!

Mr. J. H. H. FOLEY has declared that he did not go to KINGSWINFORD WORKHOUSE and PULL THE PLUGS OUT OF THE BEER BARRELS to prevent the Poor from having the Beer.

HUMBUG!

If he did not Pull the Plugs out HIMSELF, HE ORDERED the Housekeeper to pull them out, and I solemnly declare he DID GO to the Workhouse and did

Prevent the Poor from having the Beer.

and that he would not leave the Workhouse until EVERY DROP WAS MADE-AWAY WITH. ASK Mr. and Mrs. JEFCOATE IF THIS BE NOT TRUE, who were Governor and Matron of the Workhouse at the same time.

In the Barrel of Ale in the Cellar I sat,
When FOLEY came there with his Horsewhip and Hat;
With rage he was foaming, I can swear it is true,
He cried pull out the COCK—I cried *Doodle Doo!*

JACK SPIGOT.

Kingswinford Workhouse,
July 7th, 1837

THOMAS DANKS, PRINTER, HIGH STREET DUDLEY.

more tea and sugar to coat it. A cup of hot, fresh tea was soon made by dropping a ball of this mixture into an enamel mug of boiling water.

It was not uncommon for children to be sent straight from school at midday to 'take dinners' to their fathers at work. Hot, nourishing food was put in a basin and covered with a plate, on top of which was placed a chunk [ommuck] of bread and the complete meal was then covered with a cloth or very often a man's red and white spotted handkerchief, the finished result resembling a pudding ready for steaming. Meals were also taken to men working nightshifts, where the children lingered to watch the men at work on the furnaces. One such small furnace in the Rowley Regis area was appropriately nicknamed The 'Flash and Fly'.

Men, however, could soon conjure up a substantial meal for themselves of bacon and eggs cooked in the furnace on a shovel, known as a [scoven] in some areas. With such large families and a meagre income men could ill-afford to smoke the popular tobacco mixtures of the day like 'Twist', 'Pigtail', 'Nailrod', 'Old Friend', 'Black Jack', 'Red Bell', 'Black Bell' and 'Atlantic Shag', but mixtures of tea and dried leaves of rose bay willow herb were often substituted. Fresh leaves and even used tea leaves dried out were also smoked.

As men were considered to be the main breadwinners, it was accepted without question that whatever the family budget, they were entitled to a drink of beer after work, but many, unable to afford more than one pint, would supplement the volume by first filling their bellies with water. Pubs were dotted everywhere and remained open from six in the morning until late at night. Constant battles waged between chapels and pubs for the salvation of souls but men on their way to work were often tempted to call for a quick drink then stayed all day, which resulted in severe hardshop for their families. Most of the wages earned, however, were mortgaged for necessities and after paying weekly debts, there was very little left for luxuries.

Food and clothing was often obtained through the 'Tommy Shop' or on the strap, that is, items were paid for on a weekly basis over a set period of time. Beer could also be purchased by a similar system but known as 'on the slate', where a person's name and the debt he owed was chalked up on to a slate behind the pub bar for all and sundry to see, in the vain hope that this would encourage the debt to be cleared

Reproduced from the Dudley Almanack

quickly. Pawnbrokers flourished, moonlight flits were commonplace and there was a constant dread of ending up in the workhouse [workus]. Superstition prevailed and women were fearful [frit to jeth] of refusing to buy goods from travelling gypsies lest a curse was put on the family. Horseshoes were secured over doors on outside walls for good luck.

Pub brawls were commonplace as rival workers clashed but children still gathered outside some of the less disreputable pubs in the summer evenings. With the windows open they could join in sing-songs and hear snippits of local gossip. Interspersed between games of cards, dominoes and bunt-the-ring, politics were discussed, as the perennial conflict between workers and their employers gave rise to an increasing radical element, but the majority of men adopted a complacent acceptance of their day-to-day existence. There was little opportunity to air their grievances about poor working conditions, so any rancour was reserved for their evenings together. Sadly, a high percentage of people less able to cope with a life which promised nothing more than drudgery and poverty, and seeing no solution to the problem, committed suicide by hanging themselves, throwing themselves into the nearest 'cut' or marlhole, or slashing their throats with an open razor (cut throat) which, unfortunately was readily accessible in most households, hanging at the side of the fireplace in the kitchen.

Tradespeople visited most villages daily including white bonneted women who went from door to door selling blocks of salt, bundles of watercress, and pikelets (crumpets); gypsies selling homemade clothes pegs, lucky charms and artificial flowers; men selling cakes from a tray suspended around their necks; knife grinders; chimney sweeps and tinkers, but the most popular visitor was the rag and bone man. With his horse-drawn cart loaded with scrap iron and old clothing, a few feeble notes on his bugle and his cry of ["Anny ode rags"] instantly

---

A QUARREL AND ITS SEQUEL.

Charles Watson, landlord of the Old House at Home, Halford's Lane, Smethwick, and Eliza Watson, his wife, were charged at the Smethwick Police Court on Wednesday, with being drunk on certain premises, licensed for the sale of intoxicating liquors. —Sergeant Shaffery stated that he visited the Old House at Home in company with Police-constable Myatt at 10.30 p.m. on the 1st of April. He found the landlord and his wife drunk. He spoke to the former who denied the assertion of the officer. Mrs. Watson was sitting on the sofa and he, witness, accused her of being drunk. Cross-examined by Mr. J. Sharpe : Witness went to the house in consequence of a complaint he received from a police-constable. He was not aware that the daughter of defendants had complained at the Police Station that her father and mother had been quarrelling. He did not notice that Mrs. Watson's arm was scratched, but saw blood on her apron. Neither of the defendants appeared in the least excited, the male defendant was standing in the bar whilst the female appeared quite incapable of standing up. —Police-constable Myatt visited the house at 7.30 on the day in question in company with Police-constable Bradbury. He found both the landlord and his wife in a state of intoxication. He again visited the premises at 10.30 in company with Sergeant Shaffery, and could quite corroborate the evidence of that officer. —Police-constable Bradbury gave similar evidence. —Mr. Sharpe, after speaking to the good character borne by the male defendant, said his client had only partaken of three pints of beer the whole day. Both had been quarrelling, and were excited when the police paid their visit. There was no disturbance in the house, but on the other hand defendant was conducting his business in a proper manner. —Charles Watson, in answer to Mr. Sharpe, said he had conducted the house for ten years. He had had " words" with his wife on the day in question, and they had " wrestled together." He emphatically denied being drunk. —Mary Watson said the quarrel was more severe than any they have had in thirty-four years. She always had her " drop of beer " at 11 in the morning and a drop after dinner. —In answer to Superintendent Whitehouse, witness said she had had three glasses of beer during the day, "Which was quite as much as any woman should take." She sent for the police because she expected they would " frighten the bother away." The excitement was not induced by the little drink they had had, because she was just the same after she had had a little drop as before. It was a nice thing if a woman 53 years of age couldn't have half a pint of beer— (laughter). —Sergeant Shaffery, recalled, in answer to the Bench, said when he charged defendant with being drunk he replied, " I don't think I am."— Charles Watson was fined 10s. and costs, and the charge against the wife was dismissed.

From 'The Midland Sun' Saturday April 15th 1893

THE TOMMY SHOP

In 1831 the payment of wages in notes and coin of the realm was made compulsory and truck was thereby made illegal, but this practice flourished for very many years in the Black Country after 1831.

The tommy shop was usually owned by the proprietor or lessee of the mine and not by the butty. There was truck in other industries as well as mining e.g. nails. By 1842 the mining tommy shops were confined to Wolverhampton, Bilston, Darlaston· and Wednesbury. To give an example, a man was not paid for 7 or 8 weeks; during that time he drew supplies from the tommy shop. The difference between prices at an ordinary shop and a tommy shop was calculated as follows:

	Tommy Shop	Ordinary shop
Cheese	8d. lb.	5d. lb
Bacon	8d. lb.	5½d lb.
Salt butter	1/-d. lb.	9d. lb.
Tea	5d. oz.	3½d. oz.

One woman told how her lodger had to pay her in tommy because that was how he was paid. The tommy shop was a mile away. It was only open one day a week between 4 and 5 a.m. Another woman gave evidence concerning the tommy shop of Banks of Bilston. She said that there was always a dozen people waiting at the shop and they were never allowed inside. Sometimes 200 women were fighting to get in. Banks' shop was worse since young Mr. Charles Banks came to the shop. He swears at the women and is a shocking little dog.

Banks of Bilston paid wages every two weeks in tommy. Men were frightened to complain for fear of losing their jobs.

Even where wages were paid in coin of the realm workers often had to spend part of it at the tommy shop otherwise they would be sacked. A pikeman at Ward's of Bilston gave evidence that a man named Grainger had been sacked for not buying at the tommy shop.

Tommy was popular — and at times necessary — with employers because it saved capital. One manager stated that goods for the tommy shop were bought on six months credit and he could get £5,000 per annum if he could force all his workers to use the tommy shop. Mr. Baldwin, an ironmaster and magistrate, said that an employer paying £500 a week in wages would save £2,500 per annum by running a tommy shop.

(Summarised from the Midland Mining Commission 1843.)

Reproduced from the
Dudley Almanack

transformed him into a 'Pied Piper'. Children came running out of their homes armed with old clothing and anything they could cadge from their mothers in the hope that they would soon be the proud possessors of a balloon on a stick, a paper windmill, a goldfish in a jam jar, a stick of rock, or a day old chick which would then be taken home and reared on the hearth in a flannel-lined box in front of the fire.

Women played a subordinate role in society and amongst other restrictions were discouraged from frequenting public houses. Occasionally, however, some wives were permitted to fetch a jug of draught beer, served from a hatch in the outdoor of the local pub, to drink with their bread and cheese suppers. Whilst there they would often "sneak one on the sly". The following supper snacks were an alternative to bread and cheese.

NAIL MAKING

This is one of the oldest trades in the Midlands. It is carried on in Dudley, Sedgley, Gornal, Coseley, Wombourn, Wordsley, Netherton, Rowley, Cradley Heath, Lye Waste, Oldswinford, Stourbridge, Halesowen, Tipton, Oldbury, Darlaston, Pelsall and West Bromwich.

The work is carried out in workshops attached to the houses of the work people. Nail masters open warehouses in the towns and workers collect iron each week and return the nails that they have made in the preceding week.

Nailmasters meet each week to regulate wages and prices. This has continued since before 1800. Children usually start with their parents at the age of 9. Most districts make different kinds of nails. Two of the greatest difficulties of this trade are the fluctuations in the price of iron (the highest since 1800 has been £21 per ton and the lowest £4-17-6d) and competition with machine made nails.

Machine made nails began to be made about 1830 and a 1" machine made nail now sells for $\frac{1}{5}$ the price of a hand made nail.

Wages were reduced in 1837, 1838 and 1842 and in that year was the great nail strike. Since 1842 there have been constant strikes in the nail trade due to reduced wages and the tommy shop. The truck system only developed after 1830 but more than half the nails are now taken to the tommy shop, sometimes for every meal. Earnings in the best times were 12/d. to 16/-d a week, but now many cannot earn 10/-d. Before 1830 there were 50,000 workers in the nail trade but now it is down to 20,000. These 20,000 people are badly fed, badly clothed and degraded by a system which is a disgrace to England.

The horse and mule shoe nail trade is a separate branch of the trade which is more prosperous because horse shoe nails need the best quality iron and cannot be produced by machine. The average wage at the moment is between 22/-d. and 25/-d. a week.

(Summarised from an article by Ephraim Ball in the book "Birmingham and the Midland Hardware Trade" 1865)

THE SOUP
KITCHEN
WILL BE
RE-OPENED
AT
THE SHAMBLES
ON
TUESDAY, JANUARY 17TH, 1871,
AT TEN O'CLOCK,
AND ON EVERY
TUESDAY AND FRIDAY,
TILL FURTHER NOTICE.
BY ORDER,
N. HINGLEY,

CODDLED CHEESE

1 pt milk
¾ lb grated cheese
2 large onions chopped or minced roughly
Salt and pepper to taste

Place the onions, cheese and warmed milk into a basin and bake in a slow oven for about two hours. This dish is then ready to serve (when the cheese has completely melted), with crusty bread and butter. A very tasty supper dish.

CHEESE PUDDING

3 tablespoons breadcrumbs
3 tablespoons grated cheese
1 egg
1 teacupful of milk
Salt and pepper
A small knob of butter
A pinch of mixed herbs

Mix all the ingredients together and pour into a buttered pie dish. Bake in a moderate oven until nicely browned.

SAVOURY BAKE

2 or 3 medium-sized onions
½ lb sliced cheese
½ lb chopped bacon
1 oz butter

Peel and slice the onions and sauté gently in the butter until softened. (Originally these were placed in an oven to cook slowly for about one hour). Add the slices of cheese and the raw, chopped bacon. Return the dish to the oven and bake until the cheese has melted and the bacon crisp. Serve with crusty bread.

31st OCTOBER 1894
Swimming Gala at the Baths to defray the cost of damage to the Musical Instruments by the collapse of the Band Stand at the Sports on September 26th.

Reproduced from the Dudley Almanack

SAVOURY CRUNCHIES

4 oz short crust pastry
2 oz toasted oatmeal
1 oz melted margarine
1 oz grated cheese
Pepper, salt and mustard to season
Milk to mix

Roll the pastry into a length 10 x 2½ inches and place on a baking tin. Mix the oatmeal, margarine, cheese and seasoning with milk to make a fairly stiff paste and spread on the pastry. Bake in a hot oven for about twenty minutes. Cut into fingers to serve.

Icebreaking on the Canal—see page 155

Engine House, alongside the cut

The Cut

In the few leisure hours they had, families strolled through the surrounding lanes and meadows or sauntered along the towpaths of the 'cut' as the canal was popularly known. The close network of canals stretching throughout the Black Country had a longer mileage than the Grand Canal in Venice and provided an indispensible link both for the transportation of raw materials such as coal, ironstone, clay, copper, aluminium, resin, pig-iron, bulk tar and paraffin for use in candlemaking and also goods ranging from domestic items such as soap, tea, flour, wheat and sugar.

Factories were built close to the canal side for easy transportation of goods so there was a constant flow of boats carrying cargoes of differing commodities. Hops, malt and barley were delivered to

EUPHRATES PACKET
from TIPTON *to* BIRMINGHAM
In Two Hours

ON MONDAYS, THURSDAYS & SATURDAYS

for the accommodation of Passengers & conveyance
of Parcels.

Leaves M.ʳ Josʰ Aston's Factory Bridge, Tipton at ¼ past 8 o Clock in the
morning, through Tipton Green, Dudley Port, Tividale, Oldbury, Spon Lane,
Smethwick & Winson Green to M.ʳ R.ᵈ Heathcote's Waggon & Horses, Friday Bridge
Birmingham, & returns at 5 o Clock the same Evenings.

	1ˢᵗ Cabin	2 Cabin		1ˢᵗ Cabin	2ᵈ Cabin
Tipton, M.ʳ Josʰ Aston's			Oldbury, M.ʳ W. Bollards	1	9
—— M.ʳ Ja.ˢ Aston's & ⎬	1·6	1	Spon Lane, M.ʳ Ed.ᵈ Rudges	9	6
Dudley Port, M.ʳ Ed.ᵈ Williams's ⎭			Smethwick, M.ʳ Tho.ˢ Scotts	6	4½

Thomas Monk *Proprietor*

May be had for Parties, Tuesdays, Wednesdays &
Fridays.

Crosswells Brewery in Oldbury and beer carried from the brewery for distribution to the many pubs around the Black Country. Regular cargoes of chocolate crumb, a process made from evaporated milk, sugar and powdered cocoa beans, started their journey from a factory in Knighton, Shropshire, specifically built by Cadburys for evaporating milk, and made their way through the Black Country to their destination in Bournville, Birmingham where the crumb was made into the well known brand of 'Dairy Milk' chocolate.

'Icebreaker' boats were used to clear the route for cargoes hindered by frozen canals in winter. These boats were specially reinforced at the fore-end and pulled along the towpath by several horses harnessed

Roses & Castles — B.C.M.

with ropes attached to large rings down the sides of the boat. While the horses pulled, the crew of a dozen or so men rocked the boat from side to side which in turn created shockwaves, breaking the ice into slabs which were subsequently removed, leaving a clear channel for the boats to continue their journeys.

Gaily painted and decorated horsedrawn narrowboats were a familiar sight cruising through the tranquil, albeit polluted waters. The boat people were a close-knit community with a way of life and traditions of their own. Their style of dress was plain but heavily embroidered or pin-tucked bonnets with a protective covering over the eyes and neck from the sun was a distinctive part of the clothing worn by the women.

Life on the 'cut' was equally hard and the few family possessions were highly treasured. An area approximately ten to twelve feet long by seven feet wide seems inadequate space to rear a family, plus dog, cat and a caged bird but this is how the boat people lived: the remainder of the space being allocated to cargo.

The cabin surprisingly housed a cooking range, folding table, two beds, one with a locker underneath, and shelves and cupboards in every conceivable space. Despite these cramped conditions, great pride was taken in the appearance of the living quarters. A new art form emerged in the shape and vivid colours of the now famous 'Roses and Castles' design which was displayed not only on the outside of the cabins, the water-carrying jugs and horse-feed buckets but also helped to decorate practically every utensil inside; buckets, teapots, mugs, etcetera and along with grained woodwork, crotcheted curtains, ribbon plates and gleaming brasswork, became a unique form of canal boat decoration.

JUNE 1887

21—Celebration of Her Majesty's Jubilee throughout the Kingdom. In Dudley, the Celebrations consisted of a Treat to School Children, Illuminations, Bonfires, and General Rejoicings.

23—Dinner to the Aged Poor in celebration of the Jubilee.

23—Jubilee Dinner at the Dudley Conservative Working Men's Club.

Reproduced from the Dudley Almanack

Christmas

Christmas at the turn of the century was less commercialized than today with emphasis more on food than presents. This was the time of year when butchers' windows displayed the carcasses of sucking pigs with garlands around their necks and a rosy apple wedged in their mouths, in readiness for the Christmas festivities. A good plump cockerel served as Christmas dinner in most homes and was in many cases the only time of year that poultry was eaten except for an occasional boiling fowl. Poorer families managed with a roast rabbit.

Few families could afford a real Christmas tree but made their own version from either a holly bough or two wooden hoops retrieved from butter or cheese tubs, joined together and trimmed with brightly

Poor children having Christmas breakfast in a Cradley Heath school yard
—from the Author's own collection

157

coloured paper. Chains of similar paper secured with a flour and water paste adorned the downstairs rooms. About twelve weeks before Christmas, some mothers with small children paid a penny a week which was recorded on a card at the local sweet shop in order to have sweets put on one side as 'fillers' for Christmas stockings. These included sugar fancies, sugar mice and pigs, sticks of rainbow coloured rock and liquorice pipes. Little bundles of chocolate were hung on the Christmas tree but were supposedly not to be eaten until after twelfth night.

Most women made their own Christmas puddings adding a few threepenny pieces [Joey's] with the ingredients and it was customary for children to make a secret wish as they helped to stir. Enough puddings were made by some women to last for several months but a surprising number of families had to manage with a spiced-up version of Bread Pudding.

Reproduced from the Dudley Almanack

Domestic Remedies

[When yome feelin middlin]

Before the advent of the National Health Service, the working-class could ill afford to seek the help of a doctor for anything other than a serious complaint and relied on their limited knowledge of homemade remedies made from simple inexpensive ingredients and herbs supplemented by patent medicines obtained from the chemist. Most of the remedies were reliable but quite a few patent medicines contained drugs such as laudanum and were found at a later date to be extremely harmful especially those concocted for babies and little children. The following are a few of the remedies in constant use at that time.

A basin of small pieces of bread or toast, with hot milk, a little sugar and a knob of butter added was given to invalids as this was easily digested and known as 'sop'.

Sugar lumps soaked in brandy and wrapped in a covering of rag with the end knotted was given to a fractious baby to suck in a desperate attempt to stop it crying.

Bruised comfry leaves applied to a sprain helped to ease the swelling.

A handful of nettles washed thoroughly and added to the water when cooking cabbage was considered to make for longevity and this would have had a measure of truth in it as the astringent leaves of nettles contain more iron than spinach and quantities of Vitamins A and C together with important acids, nitrogen and trace elements are also

159

present. A tonic made from an infusion of the leaves was supposed to help in the treatment for anaemia, blood impurities, retention of urine, indigestion and skin diseases and also to improve circulation. The sting of the nettle is rendered harmless when boiled or dried.

The syrup from a sliced onion, layered alternatively with demerara sugar was used to cure a cough.

A small amount of boiled onion placed in a piece of muslin and applied to the ear helped to relieve earache, (the centre of the onion was used as this was the hottest part after boiling).

The skin lying immediately below the shell on a boiled egg was applied to boils to help draw pus. Another method for drawing boils was to fill a small bottle with very hot water until the bottle was hot, the water would then be poured out and the aperture placed over the boil and lightly pressed, creating a suction action — excruciatingly painful!

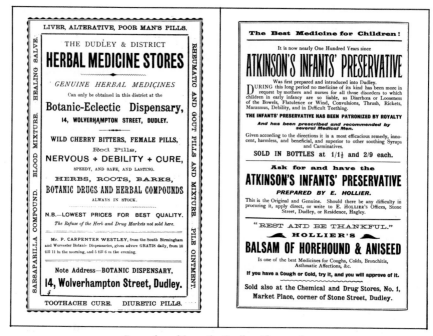

Reproduced from the Dudley Almanack

160

The milky substance from the stems of dandelions was used to clear up warts, and broth made from dandelion flowers was believed to relieve consumption.

Burnt toast (the blacker the better) was broken up and soaked in water. This mixture was taken to relieve the pains of pleurisy.

A tonic wine to "Cure all ills" but anaemia in particular was made from the following recipe:

> 6 lbs raw beetroot
> 3 lbs demerara sugar
> ½ pint old ale or guinness

Wash the beetroot and slice into a bowl. Sprinkle the sugar over. Leave for two days then strain off the liquid and mix with the ale. A tablespoonful to be taken three times daily.

Cold tea was used to bathe tired or sore eyes and fresh spring water was commonly used for the same ailment.

Raw onion or a 'blue bag' used in the weekly wash to help whiten clothes was used to treat wasp and bee stings, dock leaves being used for nettle stings.

Pitch (obtained from workmen repairing roads) was chewed to help sufferers of whooping cough and catarrh.

A mixture of brimstone and treacle was taken at monthly intervals to help clear the blood and system, and regular doses of Parrishs's Food and Epsom Salts were taken for the same purpose.

A substitute for Gripe Water given to babies to alleviate wind was Glede Water made from a red-hot ember [glede] from the fire, plunged into a little water.

Salt and soot combined, was used as tooth powder.

Goose fat was eaten to combat coughs and colds and it was quite common for some children to be rubbed all over with fat before having brown paper slapped on their back and chest and then sewn into garments to help retain heat at the onset of winter. These were not usually removed until the Spring!

Wintergreen rubbed on to the chest and covered with a piece of soft cloth (usualy flannel) brought warmth and comfort to chest sufferers. Silk stockings or a silk scarf were also placed around the neck to ease a sore throat and particular benefit was supposedly derived from an unwashed sock!

To relieve the pain from a stye [powke] on the eye, a gold wedding ring was rubbed gently over the eye but a more common practice in the Black Country was to bathe them with a decoction made from a plant which flourished on the roofs of brewhouses and was known as 'House Eye Green' or 'Eyebright'.

Rheumatism could supposedly be cured by placing a potato in the pocket of a garment worn by the sufferer and leaving it there until it became rock-hard.

A cold key was put down a persons back suffering from a nose bleed and it was firmly believed that bleeding could be stopped and healing would result by placing a spider's web over an open wound.

OLDBURY POLICE COURT.

Before Messrs. Heaton, Bennett, and Wilson.

A BROTHERLY QUARREL.—Richard and Benjamin Butcher were charged with creating a disturbance in the high road on March 25th at 7.30 p.m.—Police-cons'able Sherwood deposed to finding the brothers engaged in a stand-up fight with a crowd of specta-tors round them.—Defendants were bound over on sureties of £5 each to keep the peace for three months.—The same penalty was inflicted on William Lowe and William Baker, who were discovered late at night on the 24th of March fighting in a field near Langley Green.

DRUNKENNESS. — There were several cases of drunkenness dealt with, the majority of which were dismissed with the option of a half-crown fine or seven days' hard labour. Mary Mathews, who was charged with being drunk on April 4th on the licensed premises known as the Royal Oak, kept by Moses Mann, was discharged.

ASSAULTING THE POLICE. — George Rogers was charged with being drunk and disorderly on April 1st, and also with assaulting Police-constable Bibb.—The policeman gave evidence to the effect that he found the defendant very drunk in Birmingham Street on the night in question. A crowd had gathered round him, and he was creating a great disturbance. The defendant gave him a severe blow on the head, and kicked him repeatedly all the way down to Church Street.—The prisoner in his defence admitted being drunk, but denied that he kicked the constable. The policeman was the first to strike a blow.—The prisoner was fined 2s. 6d. and costs for each offence.

From 'The Midland Sun' Saturday April 15th 1893

BLACKCURRANT VINEGAR

Place three pounds of blackcurrants and a quart of water into a stewjar and cook in a slow oven for several hours. Leave it until it has completely cooled. Strain off the syrup and to every gallon add three pounds of light brown sugar and one quart of vinegar. Boil for about twenty minutes, skim well and when cool, bottle for use. This was good for soothing sore throats and hoarseness.

SURFEIT WATER

1 oz Cinnamon Sticks
1 lb loaf sugar
1 oz cloves
A little aniseed

Put the cloves and cinnamon sticks into a saucepan and simmer gently for about one and a half hours. Strain, add the sugar, aniseed and boiling water to make up to a quart. Cool and bottle. Surfeit water was obtainable from pubs and was taken regularly by expectant mothers as this supposedly helped at childbirth.

An infusion of raspberry leaves and boiling water drunk during pregnancy and at the commencement of labour supposedly relieved childbirth pains.

COUGH MIXTURE

4 lbs ripe elderberries
8 pints water
½ oz cloves
½ oz dried chillies
Sugar
Cinnamon sticks

Boil the elderberries in the water and add the cloves and chillies. Simmer for one hour. Strain and add 1 lb of sugar for every pint of liquid. Boil quickly until reduced and thickened. Bottle with a stick of cinnamon to each bottle. Use a tablespoonful in hot water for chesty coughs.

Black Country family group

IER CLARKE,

STO

NEW HAWNE MINERS,
NEW BRITISH IRON COMPANY,
1st AUGUST. 1872.

Class Distinction

Class distinction at the turn of the century was very pronounced with many unscrupulous employers outrageously exploiting their work force, but oppression isn't the whole story. Not enough tribute is paid to the many people, clergymen, doctors and teachers, truly mindful of the needs and welfare of the less fortunate. These people *did* exist, many giving up social positions to offer their professional expertise, often risking their own health and in some cases reducing their own wealth considerably in an effort to ease the plight of the less fortunate groups of this complex society. One of the most renowned of these was Sister Dora.

About the time when the window blinds of Queen Victoria's railway coach were drawn to hide the hideous view of the Black Country, blinds were being drawn for a very different reason in the homes of the inhabitants of Walsall. It was Saturday 28th December, 1878. Shops were closed and work came to a standstill as tribute was paid at the funeral of Dorothy Pattison, better known to the people of the Black Country and Walsall in particular as Sister Dora, who had died four days earlier.

Dorothy Pattison, born on 16th January, 1832 in the village of Hawkwell in Yorkshire, arrived in the Black Country on 8th January 1865 and devoted much of the remainder of her life to the welfare and care of the people of Walsall who came to revere her as another Florence Nightingale. 'Sister Dora' was originally a pet name from childhood and adopted later in 1864 when she entered the Christ Church sisterhood at an Anglican Convent near Middlesborough. When arriving in the Black Country she was appalled at the suffering of the lower social classes and the lack of hospital facilities available to them.

Prior to her arrival, the town's countless industrial accident cases were sent to the Birmingham Hospital by cart or rail, many dying enroute, but two years before she arrived, a small Cottage Hospital with just four beds was set up at No 4 Bridge Street, Walsall in an attempt to alleviate the suffering of the sick. Over the next few years the hospital expanded and despite the overcrowded conditions, the death rate amongst the accident victims was under five per cent compared with

TWO VIEWS OF EMPLOYERS ON CONDITIONS IN FACTORIES

1. Mr Sidney Cartwright of Cartwright & Evans, Dudley Road, Wolverhampton.

This is the only manufactory for tin toys in the kingdom. The persons employed are chiefly women and girls. The work is light, consisting of working the presses which cut and shape the tin. I should have no difficulty in getting children about ten years of age if the law were to prevent their being employed under that age but would it be wise or right to prevent parents employing their children? I am of the opinion that there is too great a tendency in these days to interfere with the industrial habits of the people. These philanthropical interferences induce a considerable amount of insubordination among the labouring population. These theorists are ignorant of the difficulties affecting the working classes and ignorant of the difficulties of employers. Competition these day is so extremely keen that profits in many cases are so reduced that they are not sufficient employers to meet their engagements. Consider for example the circumstances of a workman with 6 children. His wages would not average more than £1 a week. His family would be too expensive for him to maintain without the earnings of his children. I am strongly of the opinion that all children should be taught reading writing and the first rudiments of arithmetic and after that they should be left to their own resources. In my opinion, if children are educated too highly at first they are unfitted for labour which is so necessary in a country which is so highly taxed as this is.

2. Mr. Matthew Tildesley of Harper and Tildesley's, Willenhall.

Nearly all the boys under 13 in our works are employed by the men. Their wages vary from 2/-d to 5/-d. There are plenty of boys of this age to be got. We are very desirous that the children should be educated, but there is no system that we are aware of by which we could carry that object out without the assistance of the law. Our hours are now from 6 a.m. to 7 p.m. We did try to reduce them from 6 to 6 and then from 6 to 5-30. We carried on these hours for 5 or 6 years but no one followed us in the town and our piecework men complained that they had not enough time to do their work in and the children were nearly all employed by them. So we were compelled to return to the old system, though I believe we got as much work done with the short hours.

(Children's Employment Commission 1862)

six percent in the big London Teaching Hospitals. Eventually in 1867 a larger residence in Walsall called 'The Mount' was converted into a hospital, making facilities marginally better.

Sister Dora is remembered for her devotion and compassion to both the victims and their families in the many mine and furnace disasters of the time, the most notable being the Pelsall Colliery disaster in November 1872 when twenty-two men were cut off by flood water for five days, eventually dying of starvation and exposure. During the smallpox epidemics of 1868 and 1875 she earned the undying gratitude

Black Country Miners in cage about to descend—by kind permission of Basil Poole

of the masses by nursing those who had been struck down by the disease. She regularly dealt with mangled limbs and amputations and often clashed with local surgeons too eager to remove limbs when she knew it was possible to save them.

On 15th October 1875, she was informed of a terrible accident which had occurred at the blast furnaces of Jones and Son at Green Lane, Walsall and immediately prepared beds and medical help for the

Author's aunt. A teacher but also spent some time as a private nurse to her grandmother (sister of Sir Alfred Hickman) when she retired to Cheltenham in the early 1900's.

unfortunate victims burned in the explosion. Eleven men were engulfed in molten lead and were described by one eye witness as "more like charred logs of wood than human beings". The sight and stench of the mens' injuries was so vile that the doctors were incessantly sick but Sister Dora nursed them non-stop for ten days, apparently impervious to such influences. Only two survived, but Sister Dora devotedly nursed and cared for the injured to the end, not going to bed for ten days. One of the local doctors said of her "Sister Dora could sit up at night and work all day with little or no rest and as far as I was able to judge was neither physically nor mentally worse for it. Her strength was super-human. I never saw such a woman".

As a result of this tragic accident she met Kenyon Jones, one of the two brothers who owned the furnaces. The ensuing months saw their friendship blossom into love. Despite the difference in age, she being fifteen years older, the effects of their romance, although destined to remain secret for many years, was evident in her youthful appearance and energy which in turn was transmitted into her work. Sadly, because of the social standards of the day, the strain of a scandal proved too much and their relationship ended. Their liaison, however, had had a profound effect on her and left her restless. Despite her private grief she continued to work tirelessly for the needs of others, performing these deeds quietly and without ostentation, never turning away from a cry of distress.

ANOTHER HORRIBLE! A MOST HORRIBLE
MINE DISASTER!

Nineteen Men & Boys Roasted to Death in an Instant of Time,

AND THREE OTHERS SERIOUSLY BURNT BY MINE GAS, at ROUND'S GREEN, TUESDAY, NOV. 17, 1846.

Ministers of Religion,
Men and Women of Humanity,
Men of Philanthropy, and Men of Science;
Mine Owners, Bailiffs, Butties, Doggies, and Miners;
Coroners, Coroners' Juries, and Gentlemen of the Law;

Can nothing be done to prevent or diminish these direful Calamities?

May not the "*Fire Damp*" be *Drawn out*, as well as *Blown out* of Pits, and may it not even be made to return to the Pit again, to Light the men therewith while working?

Is it not possible to have *Gas Ways* in Pits, as well as *Air Ways*?

Should not a Premium of £500 or £1000 be offered either by Government, Mine Owners, Working Colliers, the Scientific, or the Humane, for the discovery of an effectual method of Coal Getting without the Loss of Life?

SAMUEL COOK.

DUDLEY, NOV. 18, 1846.

Goodwin, Printer, Top of Bond-st., Dudley.

About this time her suspicions that she had cancer were confirmed but she kept the knowledge to herself, declining the offer of surgery but continuing to work to the end amongst the people of the Black Country whom she had come to love and who loved and revered her in return. For a woman who had contributed so much to society, the following words written to a friend shortly before she died seem extraordinarily poignant. "I look back on my life and see nothing but leaves". She was, of course, referring to the barren fig tree of the Gospel of St. Mark, a tree destined never to produce natural fruit. Sadly, she failed to recognise that by her amazing works and selfless devotion to the needs of others, she had formed an undeniable and lasting bond with the people of the Black Country and inspired and engineered new social reforms. In 1886, a crowd of 30,000 people gathered in Walsall town centre to witness the unveiling of a life-size statue by Williamson, in her honour.

This is just one of the many examples of supreme courage and personal sacrifice which have tended to be forgotten in subsequent years.

'Butty' paying his men—by kind permission of Basil Poole

Post Office—By kind permission of Mrs M.K. Jones, Buffery Road, Dudley.
The post office at Netherton was the first one in the Midlands to receive news by morse code, of the siege of Mafeking, 11th October, 1899. People gathered from miles around to read the news

Many celebrities in industry, music, medicine, literature and athletics, had their origins in the Black Country but the majority of acclaim for the success and prosperity of this vital area of Britain at the turn of the century, without fear of contradiction, must undoubtedly go to the ordinary working-class people, born to a life of toil and labour. Without their defiant spirit surfacing time and time again against all odds, there would be no story to relate. *They were the Black Country.*

The reality and harshness of their existence was ever present, yet despite these terrible hardships, people generally enjoyed a contentment noticeably missing from todays society. Doors were rarely locked, people sang as they worked and could always be relied on to

THE EMPLOYMENT OF GIRLS

On the banks of the canals are seen many girls engaged in loading the boats with coals. These girls are substantially although coarsely clothed. The work is laborious but not beyond their strength. The clothing is obviously such that a girl cannot continue to wear it after going home. She therefore lays it aside and washes herself and puts on more agreeable clothing.

Many girls are employed under the designation of Banks Women. They stand on the bank near the mouth of a pit shaft and when a skip comes up and is lowered on to a slide they unhook it and empty the coals. They then hang an empty skip to the chain for lowering into the shaft. The wages of girls in South Staffs. are as follows:

Age	s. d.	s. d.	
12 — 13	4 0	4 6	per week
13 — 14	4 6	5 0	"
14 — 15	5 0	6 6	"
15 — 16	6 0	7 6	"
16 — 17	7 0	8 6	"
17 — 18	7 6	9 0	"

Many girls are employed on the banks of the ironstone pits in taking out the iron stone boulders from the measures in which they are contained. There are some persons who object to girls being employed outdoors in what is supposed to be laborious employment, but when we consider how many employments men have access to themselves and how few there are for women to gain their living we must be cautious not to attempt to narrow what is already limited. As to the laboriousness of their occupations, the young women are best able to judge for themselves and they are able to show that they possess a physical vigour far surpassing that of young women brought up in the close air of towns. The girls are generally singing at their work and always appear smiling and cheerful.

(Children's Employment Commission 1842)

help a neighbour in need, often sharing food and caring for each others children when times were particularly desperate; an indication perhaps that happiness is a state of mind, not entirely dependant upon circumstances or events. An expression on the lips of most Black Country working-class people in times of severe hardship or illness was [Dow gi'in] 'Don't give in' which personifies the strength of character, pluck and endurance of the fiercely proud people of this area, and speaks volumes.

Perhaps then the plain but nourishing and wholesome meals provided by the women of the Black Country compensated for the many privations families endured, and sustained them in their labours, and that the simple pastimes and treats mentioned here, brought more than a little pleasure to the children of that era.

The
"Peaceful" Cannon.

*

"Peace hath" her Victories
no less renowned
than War."

The
"Beneficent" Cannon.

*

Ever increasing the sum of
human comfort.

The
"Ubiquitous" Cannon.

*

Scattering Good(s)
the wide World o'er.

The
"Progressive" Cannon

*

Always to the Front with
Modern Improvements.

Reproduced from the Cannon Iron Foundries trade catalogue of October 1908

Westwood Press Publications

THE ROYAL TOWN of SUTTON COLDFIELD
A Commemorative History
by Douglas V. Jones

Running to 208 pages and covering the period from Saxon times up till 1974, when the Royal Town of Sutton Coldfield was amalgamated with Birmingham this is a warm human story of local people, events and landmarks.

SUTTON COLDFIELD 1974-1984 The Story of a Decade
The Modern sequel to the History of Sutton by Douglas V. Jones

A lavishly illustrated Chronicle which recalls the many changes to the face of Sutton since its merger with Birmingham, together with a Pictorial Supplement, *Sutton in 1984*.

SUTTON PARK Its History and Wildlife
by Douglas V. Jones

Profusely illustrated with a wide selection of old and new pictures most of which have not previously been published, complete with centrefold map, and detailed with three interesting walks short enough for the casual walker to take at leisure.

STEAMING UP TO SUTTON How the Birmingham to Sutton
Coldfield Railway Line was built in 1862
written by Roger Lea

Every day thousands travel on the railway line between Sutton and Birmingham, without giving much thought to its origins and history. This is the fascinating story.

THE STORY OF ERDINGTON
From Sleepy Hamlet to Thriving Suburb
by Douglas V. Jones

Tracing the history of Erdington from earliest times, through the ages up to the late twentieth century. With some ninety-eight illustrations including a period map circa 1880.

MEMORIES OF A TWENTIES CHILD
by Douglas V. Jones

A nostalgic trip into one man's childhood and youth during the years between the wars. The book is a profusely illustrated reminder of the age of steam, gas-lamps, crystal-sets and tramcars.

DURATION MAN 1939-46
My War, by Douglas V. Jones

An enthralling sequel to "Memories of a Twenties Child"

This is the story of some of those who fought the good fight against red tape, boredom and gloom in places where all three were often present. If from time to time it may appear that soldiering is a mug's game, then the reader must draw his own conclusions. 144 pages, fully illustrated.

THE BOOK OF BRUM or Mekya Selfa Tum
by Ray Tennant

Random thoughts on the dialect and accent of the Second City (Brumslang) with a glossary of the most common expressions plus Brumodes, Brumverse and Brumericks with a little more serious verse. Brilliantly illustrated with appropriate cartoons by Jim Lyndon.

Last Tram Down The Village and Other Memories of
YESTERDAY'S BIRMINGHAM
by Ray Tennant

Although all the places written about are centred in or very near to Birmingham it will, hopefully, be of interest to people who live in other cities since many of the memories could be shared and appreciated by anyone who lived through the traumatic years of the thirties and forties.